Jusuur 1

ARABIC
ALPHABET WORKBOOK

Sarah Standish | Richard Cozzens | Rana Abdul-Aziz

Georgetown University Press | Washington, DC

Library of Congress Cataloging-in-Publication Data

Names: Standish, Sarah, author. | Cozzens, Richard, author. | Abdul-Aziz, Rana, author.
Title: Jusuur 1: Arabic Alphabet Workbook / Sarah Standish, Richard Cozzens, Rana Abdul-Aziz.
Description: Washington, DC: Georgetown University Press, 2021.
Identifiers: LCCN 2021000271 | ISBN 9781647120221 (paperback)
Subjects: LCSH: Arabic alphabet. | Arabic language—Writing. | Arabic language—Textbooks for foreign speakers—English. | Arabic language—Dialects—Jordan.
Classification: LCC PJ6123.S73 2021 | DDC 492.7/11—dc23
LC record available at https://lccn.loc.gov/2021000271

♾ This paper meets the requirements of ANSI/NISO Z39.48-1992 (Permanence of Paper).

23 22   9 8 7 6 5 4 3 2
Printed in the United States of America

Cover design by Martha Madrid
Interior design by Matthew Williams, click! Publishing Services

Contents   المحتويات

	Part One	الجزء الأول
مقدمة إلى الحروف العربية	Introduction to the Arabic alphabet	2
كيفية استخدام هذا الكتاب	How to use this book	4
ب		6
ت		7
ث		10
ا		14
ي		17
و		20
مقدمة إلى حركات	Introduction to the short vowels	23
فتحة (ـَ)		24
كسرة (ـِ)		26
ضمة (ـُ)		30
أ		36

	Part Two	الجزء الثاني
ل		42
م		47
ن		50
ه		53
ي		57
و		59
ـَي		61
ـَو		63
سكون (ـْ)		65

	Part Three	الجزء الثالث
ج		72
ح		76
خ		80
ع		85
غ		91

	Part Four	الجزء الرابع
س		100
ش		105
ر		108
ز		112
ف		115
ق		118
ك		122

	Part Five	الجزء الخامس
ة		134
د		139
ذ		142
أ إ		146
شدة (ـّ)		150

	Part Six	الجزء السادس
ص		164
ض		168
ط		172
ظ		175
أ		179

الجزء السابع **Part Seven**

أُو إيـ آ 192

الـ 197

ألف لام والحروف الشمسية والقمرية 200

ئ ؤ أ ء 207

ى 211

ألف خنجرية (ـٰ) 213

تنوين (اً ـٌ ـٍ) 214

أ 218

Art credits 223
About the Authors 225

PART ONE

الجزء الأول

PART ONE GOALS

أهداف الجزء الأول

By the end of this section, you should be able to do the following:

- Identify the major features of the Arabic alphabet
- Read, write, pronounce, and connect the consonants: ب ت ث
- Read, write, pronounce, and connect Arabic's three long vowels: ا ي وِ
- Read, write, and pronounce Arabic's three short vowels: ﹻ ﹷ ﹹ
- Read, write, and pronounce the combination of *alif-hamza* and *fatHa*: أَ

INTRODUCTION TO THE ARABIC ALPHABET

مقدّمة إلى الحروف العربية

Here are the letters of the Arabic alphabet individually. What do you notice about them?

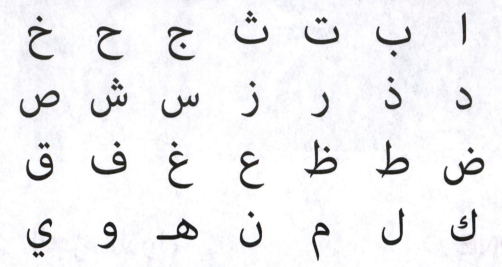

Here's an example of written Arabic. This is a line from one of the most famous poems in the Arabic language, written in the sixth century CE. What do you notice about the script?

بِسِقطِ اللِّوى بَينَ الدُّخولِ فحَوْملِ   قِفا نَبكِ مِن ذِكرى حَبيبٍ ومَنْزِلِ

Look over the letters and the example of writing. What do you observe? What jumps out at you?

What do you know about the Arabic alphabet?

ماذا تعرف عن الحروف العربية؟

Teachers: Find a printable sheet for this activity on the Jusuur website.

Read over the following true or false statements about the Arabic alphabet by yourself or with a partner. Which do you think are true and which do you think are false? Keep track on a separate piece of paper. You are not expected to know these answers; just make your best guess.

1. Arabic is written from left to right.
2. There are no uppercase and lowercase letters in Arabic.
3. Arabic uses the same alphabet as Hebrew.
4. The Arabic alphabet has fewer letters than English.
5. Like French and English, many Arabic words have silent letters.
6. Arabic words can only be written in cursive.
7. There is no *p* sound in the Arabic alphabet.
8. Arabic speakers usually do not write the short vowels on Arabic words.
9. Arabic speakers do not usually write the dots on Arabic words.
10. It is possible to type in Arabic on a computer or smartphone.
11. The Arabic alphabet can be represented in sign language.

كيفية ربط الحروف العربية

How to connect Arabic letters

As you learned earlier, Arabic is always written as cursive because Arabic words are formed by connecting letters together; a group of totally unconnected Arabic letters does not mean or say anything. To start writing in Arabic, then, there are a couple of things you need to know about how Arabic letters connect:

(1) All Arabic letters can connect, but they do so in two different ways. In this book, we will call Arabic letters "**social letters**" or "**antisocial letters**" based on the way they connect.

Social Letters	Antisocial Letters
Social letters **always** connect with the letter that comes after them. Since Arabic is written from right to left, which side will social letters **always** connect on?	Antisocial letters **never** connect with the letter that comes after them. Since Arabic is written from right to left, which side will anti-social letters **never** connect on?

(2) Every Arabic letter appears in up to **four different shapes.** The shape a letter takes depends on where the letter occurs in a word and what kind of letter comes before it.

4	3	2	1
A shape for when the letter is at the **end** of a word **after an anti-social letter** *or* when the letter is written **by itself**, as in an alphabet poster	A shape for when the letter is at the **end** of a word **after a social letter**	A shape for when the letter is in the **middle** of a word **after a social letter**	A shape for when the letter is at the **beginning** of a word *or* when the letter is in the **middle** of a word **after an anti-social letter**

Remember that even though they look different, the multiple shapes of any given letter all represent the same sound.

HOW TO USE THIS BOOK   كيفية استخدام هذا الكتاب

This book teaches the most common Arabic letters toward the beginning so that you can begin to read and write useful Arabic words as soon as possible. This book also teaches letters with similar shapes together, regardless of how often the letters are used in common words. The order in which we teach the letters also is different from the order of the alphabet, which you can see on the first page of this section.

    Until we have introduced you to all the Arabic letters, we will sometimes write Arabic words using the Latin alphabet. This is called "transliteration" and is commonly done between languages that use different scripts. Here is a guide to the letters and symbols we will use to represent Arabic letters. You do not need to master or memorize this system; it is here as a reference. (In general, it is good to avoid using transliteration, as it slows down your learning of Arabic letters.) There is no universal standard way of writing Arabic letters in the Latin alphabet. This method is the same one used in the textbook *Alif Baa* by Kristen Brustad, Mahmoud Al-Batal, and Abbas Al-Tonsi.

Transliteration Symbol	Arabic Letter	Transliteration Symbol	Arabic Letter
z	ز	aa	ا
s	س	b	ب
sh	ش	t	ت
S	ص	th	ث
D	ض	j	ج
T	ط	H	ح
DH	ظ	kh	خ
c	ع	d	د
gh	غ	dh	ذ
f	ف	r	ر

Transliteration Symbol	Arabic Letter	Transliteration Symbol	Arabic Letter
uu \ w	و	q	ق
ii \ y	ي	k	ك
a	َ	l	ل
u	ُ	m	م
i	ِ	n	ن
'	ء	h	ه

The first letter you will learn is the consonant *baa'*.

Letter name: باء (*baa'*)

Sound: *baa'* sounds like an English *b* sound. Listen to *baa'* in the following words and repeat them:

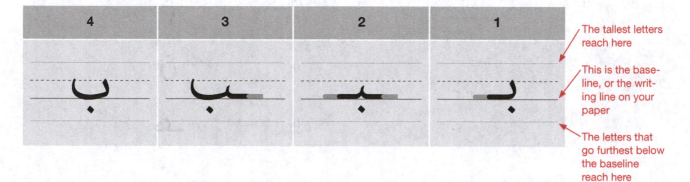

حَبيب   بَعد   بَين   كَباب

Social/antisocial: This letter is a social letter, meaning it connects to letters that come after it.

Shapes: Like most Arabic letters, *baa'* has four different shapes that make the same sound.

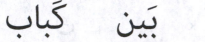

This icon means that there is an audio file on the Jusuur website.

4	3	2	1
ب	ـب ـبـ	ـبـ بـ	ـب بـ

The tallest letters reach here

This is the base-line, or the writing line on your paper

The letters that go furthest below the baseline reach here

Activity 1   Practice writing *baa'*   نشاط ١   تدريب على كتابة الباء

Practice writing each form of ب as many times as you can across one line. Practicing writing the letter helps your hands develop a muscle memory for it. The bottom edge of this letter should sit on the line, while the dot should fall under the line. Say the sound aloud as you write it.

Some people think that the dot under ب is like a **b**all that rolled under a house. What does this letter's appearance remind you of? How will you help yourself remember its sound? Draw a picture or write some notes here:

Letter name: تاء (*taa'*)

Sound: *taa'* sounds like an English *t*, pronounced with your tongue just behind your teeth. Listen to *taa'* in the following words and repeat them.

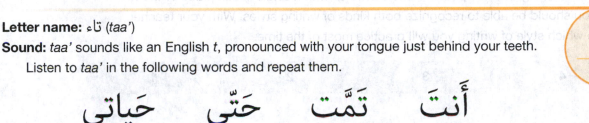

حَيَاتي   حَتّى   تَمَّت   أَنتَ

Social/antisocial: This letter is social.

Shapes: Like most Arabic letters, *taa'* takes four different shapes. You will notice that the base shapes of *taa'* are the same as the base shapes of *baa'*, but with the dots in a different place.

4	3	2	1
ت	ـت	ـتـ	تـ

Activity 2   Practice writing *taa'*

Practice writing each form of ت as many times as you can across one line. Say the sound aloud as you write it.

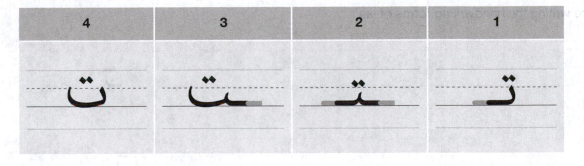

تـ

ـتـ

ت

In handwriting, Arabic speakers often write ت with a single line in place of the two dots. You should be able to recognize both kinds of writing styles. With your teacher, choose which style of writing you will practice most of the time.

4	3	2	1

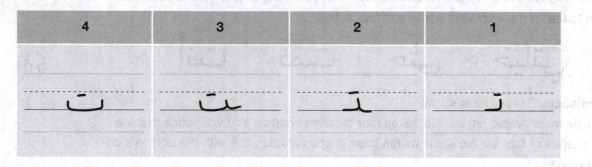

Practice writing the handwriting forms of *taa'*:

ـت

ـتـ

ـتـ

تـ

Some people remember this letter by saying that it represents a **t** sound because it has two dots. What does this letter's appearance remind you of? How will you help yourself remember its sound? Draw a picture or write some notes here:

Activity 3   Reading practice: Where are the letters? (*baa'* and *taa'*)

نشاط ٣   تدريب على القراءة: أين الحروف؟ (الباء والتاء)

The written Arabic language only came into being during the eighth century. Before then, poetry and stories were passed down orally, as was done in many traditions, and the ability to both memorize and eloquently deliver poetry was a valued skill. Poetry has been an integral part of Arab culture since even before the emergence of Islam in the seventh century. Tribes took pride in their poets representing them at competitions loosely similar to modern-day poetry slams, where they would recite from memory their own poetry on themes such as romance, the beauty of life in the desert, and the grandeur of their own tribes. Today, Arabs still consider poetry to be a key component of their cultural heritage. *American Idol*-style television shows such as أمير الشعراء (*Prince of Poets*) feature aspiring poets showcasing their eloquent Modern Standard Arabic (MSA), known as *al-fuSHaa* in Arabic. This is the variety of Arabic most often used in written and formal contexts.

Scan these lines from the poem "Don't Cry, Laila" by the classical Arab poet Abu Nuwas, born in the late eighth century. Circle each instance you see of the letters ب and ت.

واشرَب على الوَردِ من حمراء كالوَردِ   لا تَبْكِ ليلى ولا تطرَبْ إلى هندِ

أجدَتْهُ حُمْرَتَها في العينِ والخدّ   كأساً إذا انحدَرَت في حلْقِ شاربها

How many do you see of each letter? ب: _____   ت: _____

Activity 4   Letter connection practice: *baa'* and *taa'*

نشاط ٤   تدريب على ربط الحروف: الباء والتاء

In order to combine individual letters to form words, you need to connect them to each other. Choose the correct shape of the letter, according to where the letter occurs in the word (beginning, middle, or end) and whether or not it follows a social or anti-social letter pattern.

When writing each word, first complete the whole base shape for the word without lifting your pencil from the page; then go back and add the dots to all the letters.

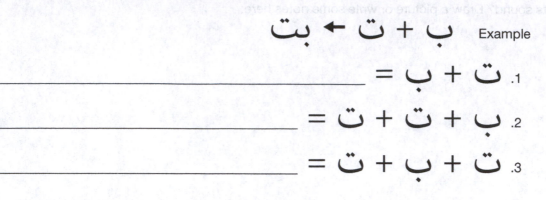

Example   بت ← ت + ب

.1   _____ = ت + ب

.2   _____ = ت + ت + ب

.3   _____ = ت + ب + ت

Note: This book will include practice writing real Arabic words to familiarize you with their look and sound, though you will not need to know the meaning of each word. At this stage, until you know a few more Arabic letters, some of the "words" you practice writing may not be real Arabic words.

Letter name: ثاء (thaa')

Sound: thaa' sounds similar to an English th, as in thing, thin, birth, and sloth. Note that this is **not** the same sound that th makes in this, clothing, and bother. Say these words aloud to hear the difference. What other English words can you think of that have the sound ث (thaa') in them? Listen to thaa' in the following words and repeat them:

ثَلاث   مِثَل   ثانِية   كَثير

Note: In some Arabic dialects, ث is pronounced with different sounds. You will learn more about this in Part Six. For now, focus on the sound it makes in Modern Standard Arabic (MSA), as described above.

Social/antisocial: This letter is social.

Shapes: thaa' is similar to baa' and taa', with four different shapes and the same base.

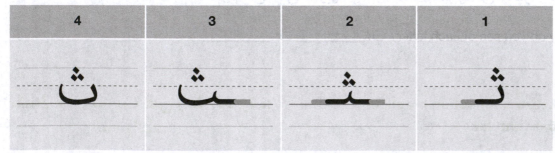

4	3	2	1
ث	ـثـ	ـثـ	ثـ

Activity 5   Practice writing *thaa'*

نشاط ٥   تدريب على كتابة الثاء

Practice writing each form of ث as many times as you can across one line. Say the sound aloud as you write it.

ث

ثــ

ــثــ

ث

In handwriting, Arabic speakers often write ث with a caret shape instead of three dots. Just like with ت, you should be able to recognize both kinds of writing styles. For this and all other letters that have different handwriting shapes, choose which style of writing you will practice most of the time.

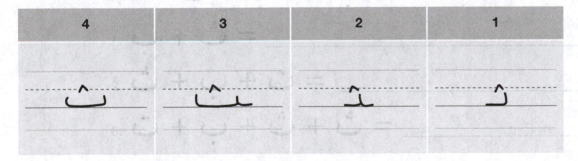

4	3	2	1

Practice writing the handwriting forms of *thaa'*:

ث

ث

What does this letter's appearance remind you of? How will you help yourself remember its sound? Draw a picture or write some notes here:

Activity 6   Letter connection practice: *thaa'*

نشاط ٦   تدريب على ربط الحروف: الثاء

Connect the letters as appropriate to form words.

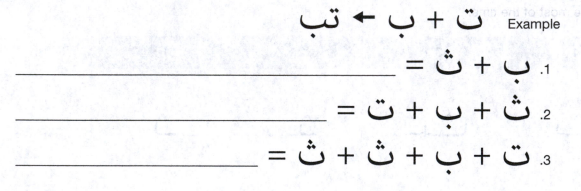

Example   تب ← ب + ت

1. ب + ث = _____

2. ث + ب + ت = _____

3. ت + ب + ث + ث = _____

Activity 7   Listening practice: *baa'*, *taa'*, and *thaa'*

نشاط ٧   تدريب على الاستماع: الباء والتاء والثاء

First listening   الاستماع الأول

The three letters ب, ت, and ث look very similar, but the dots mean they make very different sounds. Below is the independent shape for these three letters, but—oops!—someone forgot to write the dots. Listen to your teacher say different letter sounds, and write the dots on each letter correctly.

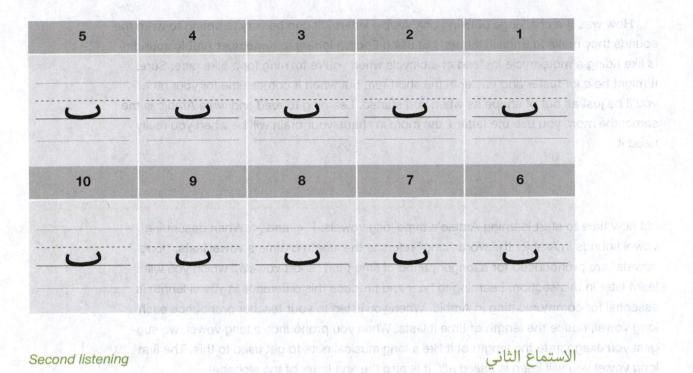

5	4	3	2	1
ب	ب	ب	ب	ب

10	9	8	7	6
ب	ب	ب	ب	ب

Second listening   الاستماع الثاني

Now do the same activity with a partner:

    Write out ten letters you want to read to your partner, in a random order. It is important that you write your letters *only* in Arabic and use your memory to recall what sounds they make as you read them aloud to your partner.

    Read them to your partner while they write down the dots correctly, then check their answers. Write down the correct dots with the letters they read out loud to you:

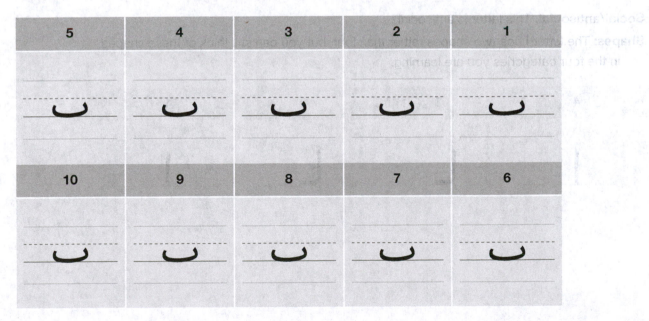

5	4	3	2	1
ب	ب	ب	ب	ب

10	9	8	7	6
ب	ب	ب	ب	ب

How was the challenge of using only Arabic letters? It can be very tempting to write the sounds they make in English letters, but using English letters to remember Arabic sounds is like riding a motorcycle instead of a bicycle when you're training for a bike race. Sure, it might be *a lot* faster and easier in the short run, but when it comes time for your race you'll be just as out of shape as when you started. Learning to read and write Arabic is the same: the more you use the letters, the more in shape your brain will be when you really need it.

It's now time to start learning Arabic's three long vowels: ا, و, and ي. When describing vowel sounds in Arabic, the word "long" refers to the length of time a vowel lasts; "long vowels" are pronounced for a longer period of time than "short vowels," which you will learn later in this section. Learning to hear and produce this difference in vowel length is essential for communicating in Arabic. When you listen to your teacher pronounce each long vowel, notice the length of time it lasts. When you pronounce a long vowel, we suggest you exaggerate the length of it like a long musical note to get used to this. The first long vowel you will learn is called *alif*. It is also the first letter of the alphabet.

Letter name: ألف (*alif*)

Sound: *alif* can make a slightly different sound depending on what other letters are around it. It usually represents an *a* sound like in *cat*, but it can also represent a "deeper" *a* sound as in *tall*. Speakers of different dialects pronounce *alif* slightly differently as well. When writing words in English letters in this book, we use "*aa*" to represent the long *alif* sound. Listen to *alif* in the following words and repeat them:

قال   ناس   واحِد   ما

Social/antisocial: This letter is antisocial.

Shapes: The letter ا has two shapes rather than four, but you can still think of these shapes in the four categories you are learning.

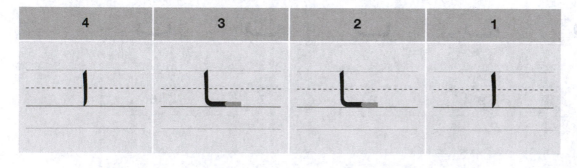

4	3	2	1
ا	ﻠ	ﺎ	ا

Activity 8   Practice writing *alif*   نشاط ٨   تدريب على كتابة الألف

Practice writing each form of ا as many times as you can across one line. When writing the second shape of *alif*, make sure that you start writing at the bottom of the letter, not at the top. This second shape always comes after a social letter, so you should practice writing it that way. Say the sound aloud as you write it.

ا

ـا

What does this letter's appearance remind you of? How will you help yourself remember its sound? Draw a picture or write some notes here:

Activity 9   Letter connection practice: *alif*

نشاط ٩   تدريب على ربط الحروف: الألف

Connect the letters as appropriate to form words.

Example   ب + ا ← با

1. ب + ا + ب + ت = _____

2. ث + ا + ب + ت = _____

3. ث + ب + ا + ت = _____

4. ت + ا + ب + ت = _____

Activity 10   Practice reading *alif*

نشاط ١٠   تدريب على قراءة الألف

Practice reading these words with ا in them out loud, and remember to make the vowel last a long time:

ثاب   بات   تابا   باب

Activity 11   Dictation practice: *alif*

نشاط ١١   تدريب على الإملاء: الألف

Listen to the words and write them in Arabic letters:

1. _____

2. _____

3. _____

4. _____

5. _____

6. _____

7. _____

8. _____

The letter *yaa'* is another of Arabic's three long vowels.

Letter name: ياء (*yaa'*)

Sound: When acting as a vowel, *yaa'* makes a long *ee* sound as in *week*. Remember that long vowels in Arabic last a long time and you should exaggerate their length as you practice. When writing Arabic words in English letters in this book, we represent the long vowel *yaa'* with the letters "*ii*." Listen to *yaa'* in the following words and repeat them:

مَدينة   في   جَديد   كَثير

Social/antisocial: This letter is social.

Shapes: Like the first three letters you learned, the letter *yaa'* has four distinct shapes. Look at the boxes below and observe how these shapes are both similar to and different from the shapes for *baa'*, *taa'*, and *thaa'*.

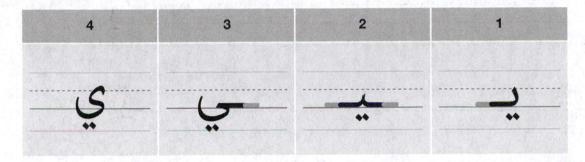

4	3	2	1
ي	ي	ـيـ	يـ

Activity 12 Practice writing *yaa'*   نشاط ١٢   تدريب على كتابة الياء

Practice writing each form of ي as many times as you can across one line. Say the sound aloud as you write it.

يـ

ـيـ

ـي

ي

As with the letter ت, it is common to write ي with a straight line instead of two dots in handwriting. Practice each of these forms across one line.

4	3	2	1
ﻱ	ﻱ	ﻴ	ﻴ

Practice writing the handwriting forms of *yaa'*:

ﻴ

ﻴ

ﻱ

ﻱ

What does this letter's appearance remind you of? How will you help yourself remember its sound? Draw a picture or write some notes here:

| نشاط ١٣ تدريب على القراءة: أين | **Activity 13 Reading practice: Where are** |
| الحروف؟ (الياء والثاء) | **the letters? (thaa' and yaa')** |

Scan these lines from the poem "*Muᶜallaqat Imri' al-Qays*" by the pre-Islamic Arab poet
Imru' al-Qays, and circle each instance you see of ث and ي:

وأنّكِ مَهما تأمُري القلبَ يفعلِ   أغرّكِ منّي أنَّ حبّكِ قاتلي

بسهمَيكِ في أعشارِ قلبٍ مُقتّلِ   وما ذرفتْ عيناكِ إلّا لتَضرِبي

How many do you see of each? ث: _____ ي: _____

| نشاط ١٤ تدريب على ربط الحروف: الياء | **Activity 14 Letter connection practice:** |
| | **yaa'** |

Connect the letters as appropriate to form words.

_____ = ب + ي + ت ١.

_____ = ب + ث + ي ٢.

_____ = ب + ي + ا + ت ٣.

_____ = ب + ت + ا + ت + ي ٤.

_____ = ت + ي + ب + ث + ت ٥.

| نشاط ١٥ تدريب على قراءة الياء | **Activity 15 Practice reading yaa'** |

Practice reading these words with ي in them out loud, and remember to make the vowel
last longer than an English *ee* sound:

ثيابي   ثيب   تيب   تيث

The third and final long vowel in Arabic is the letter *waaw.*

Letter name: واو (*waaw*)

Sound: When acting as a long vowel, *waaw* makes a long *oo* sound as in *spook* and *duke*. Remember to exaggerate the length of the long vowels. When writing Arabic words in English letters in this book, we represent the long vowel *waaw* with the letters "*uu*." Listen to *waaw* in the following words and repeat them:

أَمريكِيّون   مَشروع   سور   دون

Social/antisocial: This letter is antisocial.

Shapes: Like *alif,* the letter *waaw* has two shapes rather than four, but again, you can still think of these shapes in the four categories you learned.

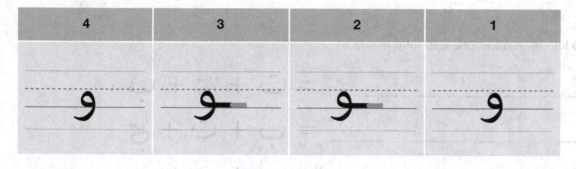

Activity 16 Practice writing *waaw*   نشاط ١٦   تدريب على كتابة الواو

Practice writing each form of و as many times as you can across one line. Remember that the loop sits *on* the line and the "tail" hangs *under* the line. Say the sound aloud as you write it.

What does this letter's appearance remind you of? How will you help yourself remember its sound? Draw a picture or write some notes here:

Activity 17 Letter connection practice: نشاط ١٧ تدريب على ربط الحروف:

waaw   الواو

Connect the letters as appropriate to form words.

ث + و + ب = _____ ١.

و + ا + و = _____ ٢.

ب + و + ا + ب = _____ ٣.

ت + و + ي + ب = _____ ٤.

ث + و + ب + ت = _____ ٥.

Activity 18 Listening practice: *alif, yaa',*   نشاط ١٨ تدريب على الاستماع: الألف

and waaw   والياء والواو

In this drill, you will listen to six words that each contain one of the long vowel sounds. For each word, write an X in the column of the long vowel sound that you hear. These words will contain letters or short vowels that you do not know; just concentrate on listening to the long vowel sounds.

و	ي	ا	
			١.
			٢.

و	ي	ا	
			.3
			.4
			.5
			.6

نشاط ١٩   تدريب على قراءة الواو   **Activity 19   Practice reading *waaw***

Practice reading these words with و in them out loud, and remember to make the vowel
last longer than the *oo* sound in English.

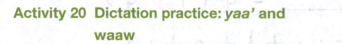

بوت   توث   توب

نشاط ٢٠   تدريب على الإملاء: الياء والواو   **Activity 20   Dictation practice: *yaa'* and**
                                                       waaw

Listen to the words and write them in Arabic letters:

_____ .1

_____ .2

_____ .3

_____ .4

_____ .5

_____ .6

نشاط ٢١   تدريب على القراءة: أين   **Activity 21   Reading practice: Where are**
الحروف؟   **the letters?**

It's time for an alphabet scavenger hunt! Below are a list of clues and lines from another
poem by the classical poet Abu Nuwas. Read each clue, then scan the poem for one
example of the letter it describes. Once you find an example, circle it and write the number
of the corresponding clue next to it. You can then cross that clue off in the scavenger hunt.

Scavenger hunt clues:

1. ا after a social letter
2. ا after an anti-social letter or at the beginning of a word
3. و after a social letter
4. و after an anti-social letter or at the beginning of a word
5. بَ at the beginning of a word or after an anti-social letter
6. ب in the middle of a word after a social letter
7. ب at the end of a word after a social letter
8. ب at the end of a word after an anti-social letter
9. ت at the beginning of a word or after an anti-social letter
10. ت in the middle of a word after a social letter
11. ت at the end of a word after a social letter
12. ت at the end of a word after an anti-social letter
13. ي at the beginning of a word or after an anti-social letter
14. ي in the middle of a word after a social letter
15. ي at the end of a word after a social letter
16. ث at the beginning of a word or after an anti-social letter

وللّذي تمزجُ شرابُ	إنّي لما سُمْتَ لرِكّابُ
من يدكَ العلقمُ والصّابُ	لا عائفاً شَيئاً ولوْ شِيتَ لي
عنْدي ولا ضرّكَ مغْتابُ	ما حطّكَ الواشون عن رتبةٍ
عليكَ عنْدي بالّذي عابُوا	كأنّما أثنوا ولم يشعروا
لسْتُ بشيءٍ منكَ أرْتابُ	وأنت لي أيضاً كذا قُدوةٌ
يَعْدَمُنا شوْقٌ وأطْرابُ	فكيْفَ يُعيينا التّلاقي وما
تكذبُ في الميعَاد كذّابُ	كأنّما أنتَ وإن لم تكنْ
جئتَ فهذا منكَ لي دَابُ	إن جئتُ لم تأتِ وإن لم أجيءْ

INTRODUCTION TO THE SHORT VOWELS

مقدمة إلى الحركات

In addition to the three long vowels in Arabic, there are three short vowels. Just as you learned to extend the length of the long vowels, you will learn to pronounce the short vowels very, very briefly. Recognizing and producing the difference between these long and short sounds is essential to communicating in Arabic.

The symbols for the short vowel sounds are written above and below the Arabic letters, giving information about how to pronounce words correctly. These short vowel symbols are not considered to be part of the Arabic alphabet.

In many situations, such as in novels, news articles, and text messages, short vowels are not written on Arabic words. This makes things tricky for beginning Arabic students—but like native Arabic speakers, you will soon get used to reading without them. For example, you can probably recognize these English words without their vowels:

hmwrk   tmrrw   schl   mnth   wrtng

There are some texts, however, in which Arabic speakers *do* write short vowels on words, such as the Qur'an, the Bible, poetry, and some textbooks and children's books. Think of these vowels as accessories that Arabic words only wear on formal occasions, the way a person wears a tie or fancy jewelry in certain situations but not in others.

Name: فتحة (*fatHa*)

Sound: *fatHa* makes a short *a* sound. The word "*fatHa*" in Arabic means "opening"; when you pronounce *fatHa*, you should make a small opening with your mouth. In this book, we will always use "*a*" to represent this vowel when writing Arabic words in English letters. Don't be afraid to overemphasize the briefness of the short vowels and length of the long vowels! Pronouncing long and short vowels correctly is one of the most important things you can do to help your Arabic pronunciation. Listen to *fatHa* in the following words and repeat them:

مَكان   شَكل   كَبير   لَم

Shape: The short vowel *fatHa* is written as a small diagonal slash *above* a letter:

بَث

The short *a* sound of the *fatHa* is pronounced immediately after the letter that it is written above. The arrows in this diagram show how to read the consonants and vowel in this word: Start with the sound of the ب, then the sound of the *fatHa*, then the sound of the ث.

Activity 22 Practice writing *fatHa*   نشاط ٢٢ تدريب على كتابة الفتحة

Practice writing the combination of different consonants and *fatHa*. Pronounce each combination as you write it. Challenge yourself by writing the consonants in each of their different shapes.

بَ

تَ

ثَ

What does this short vowel's appearance remind you of? How will you help yourself remember its sound? Draw a picture or write some notes here:

Activity 23 Listening practice: *fatHa* vs. *alif*

نشاط ٢٣   تدريب على الاستماع: الفتحة مقابل الألف

In this drill, you will listen to ten words that contain the long vowel sound ١ (*aa*), the short vowel sound ـَ (*a*), or both sounds. For each word, write an X in the column of the vowel sound that you hear, or in both if you hear both. These words will contain letters that you do not know; just concentrate on listening to the vowel sounds.

١	ـَ	
		.1
		.2
		.3
		.4
		.5
		.6
		.7
		.8

	١	ـَ	
			٩.
			١٠.

Activity 24 Practice reading *fatHa*   نشاط ٢٤ تدريب على قراءة الفتحة

Practice reading these words with *fatHa* in them out loud. Practice making the *alif* last at least twice as long as the *fatHa*.

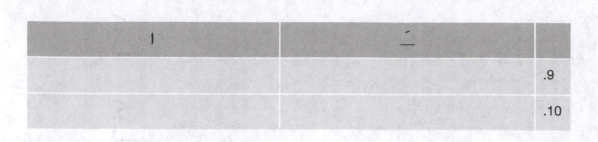

ابَت   تَبَب   بَتات   تَبتيب   بَت

Name: كسرة (*kasra*)

Sound: *kasra* represents a short *i* sound, usually pronounced like the vowel in *bit*. When it occurs at the end of a word, it can sound more like the vowel in *beet*. We will always use "*i*" to represent *kasra* in English letters. You will pronounce *kasra* very briefly, as it is a short vowel; its duration is much shorter than that of the long vowel ي. Listen to *kasra* in the following words and repeat them:

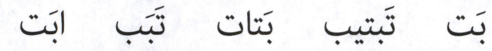

مِثلَ   كِتاب   بِكِ   مِن

Shape: The short vowel *kasra* is written as a small diagonal slash *below* a letter:

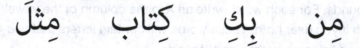

The short *i* sound of the *kasra* is pronounced immediately after the letter that it is written below. The arrows in this diagram show how to read the consonants and vowel in this word: Start with the sound of the ب, then the sound of the *kasra*, then the sound of the ث.

Activity 25 Practice writing *kasra*   نشاط ٢٥ تدريب على كتابة الكسرة

Practice writing the combination of different consonants and *kasra*. Pronounce each combination as you write it. Challenge yourself by writing the consonants in each of their different shapes.

بَ

تَ

ثَ

What does this short vowel's appearance remind you of? How will you help yourself remember its sound? Draw a picture or write some notes here:

Activity 26 Listening practice: *kasra* vs. *yaa'*

نشاط ٢٦   تدريب على الاستماع: الكسرة مقابل الياء

kasra is considered the short vowel equivalent to the long vowel *yaa'*, but it can sound surprisingly different. In this drill, you will listen to ten words that contain the long vowel sound ي (*ii*), the short vowel sound ﹺ (*i*), or both sounds. For each word, write an X in the column of the vowel sound that you hear, or in both if you hear both. These words will contain letters that you do not know; just concentrate on listening to the vowel sounds.

ي	ﹺ	
		.1
		.2
		.3
		.4

ي	ـِ	
		.5
		.6
		.7
		.8
		.9
		.10

Activity 27 Listening practice: *fatHa* vs. *kasra*

نشاط ٢٧   تدريب على الاستماع: الفتحة مقابل الكسرة

Practice hearing the difference between the two short vowels *fatHa* (*a*) and *kasra* (*i*). For each word, write an X in the column of the vowel sound that you hear, or in both if you hear both. These words will contain letters that you do not know; just concentrate on listening to the vowel sounds.

ـِ	ـَ	
		.1
		.2
		.3
		.4
		.5
		.6
		.7
		.8
		.9
		.10

Activity 28   Practice reading *kasra*   نشاط ٢٨   تدريب على قراءة الكسرة

Practice reading these words out loud, making your pronunciation of long vowels last at least twice as long as that of short vowels.

بِتْ   تِبْ   باتِتْ   ثابِت

Activity 29   Listening practice: Which short vowel?   نشاط ٢٩   تدريب على الاستماع: أي حركة؟

The following words do not have any short vowels written on them. Listen and write the short vowels that you hear above or below the correct letter.

باتت .1

تابت .2

تثبيت .3

تبتي .4

Name: ضمة (*Damma*)

Sound: *Damma* makes a short *u* sound. This sometimes sounds like the *u* in *put* and sometimes like the *oo* in *boot*. We will always use "*u*" to represent *Damma* in English letters. You will pronounce *Damma* very briefly, as it is a short vowel; its duration is much shorter than that of the long vowel و. Listen to these syllables and words that contain *Damma* and practice saying them aloud.

حُقوق   رَجُل   طُرُق   ثُمَّ

Shape: The short vowel *Damma* is written as a small, looped ribbon *above* a letter:

بُث

The short *u* sound of the *Damma* is pronounced immediately after the letter that it is written above. The arrows in this diagram show how to read the consonants and vowel in this word: Start with the sound of the ب, then the sound of the *Damma*, then the sound of the ث.

Activity 30 Practice writing *Damma*   نشاط ٣٠   تدريب على كتابة الضمة

Practice writing the combination of different consonants and *Damma*. Pronounce each combination as you write it. Challenge yourself by writing the consonants in each of their different shapes.

بُ

تُ

ثُ

What does this short vowel's appearance remind you of? How will you help yourself remember its sound? Draw a picture or write some notes here:

Activity 31 Listening practice: *Damma* vs. *waaw*

نشاط ٣١ تدريب على الاستماع: الضمّة مقابل الواو

Damma is considered the short vowel equivalent to the long vowel *waaw*; even when the two sound similar, *Damma* is much shorter. In this drill, you will listen to ten words that contain the long vowel sound و (*uu*), the short vowel sound ُـ (*u*), or both sounds. For each word, write an X in the column of the vowel sound that you hear, or in both if you hear both. These words will contain letters that you do not know; just concentrate on listening to the vowel sounds.

و	ُـ	
		.1
		.2
		.3
		.4
		.5
		.6
		.7
		.8
		.9
		.10

Activity 32 Practice reading *Damma*   نشاط ٣٢ تدريب على قراءة الضمة

Practice reading these words out loud, making your pronunciation of long vowels last at least twice as long as that of short vowels.

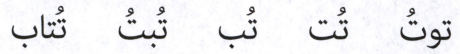

تُتاب   تُبتُ   تُب   تُت   توتُ

Activity 33 Listening practice: *fatHa, kasra,* and *Damma*   نشاط ٣٣ تدريب على الاستماع: الفتحة والكسرة والضمة

In this drill, you will listen to fifteen one-syllable words that contain one of the three short vowel sounds: ــَ (a) ــِ (i) ــُ (u). For each word, write an X in the column of the vowel sound that you hear in that word. These words will contain letters that you do not know; concentrate on listening to the short vowel sounds.

ــُ	ــِ	ــَ	
			١.
			٢.
			٣.
			٤.
			٥.
			٦.
			٧.
			٨.
			٩.
			١٠.
			١١.
			١٢.
			١٣.
			١٤.
			١٥.

Activity 34 Listening practice: *fatHa,*
**   *kasra, Damma, alif, waaw, yaa'***

نشاط ٣٤   تدريب على الاستماع: فتحة،
كسرة، ضمة، ألف، واو، ياء

In this drill, you will listen to fifteen words, each of which is made up of two syllables. Write down the two vowels that you hear in each word in the order that you hear them. Remember to listen for whether the vowels are long or short. The six Arabic vowels are printed below for your reference.

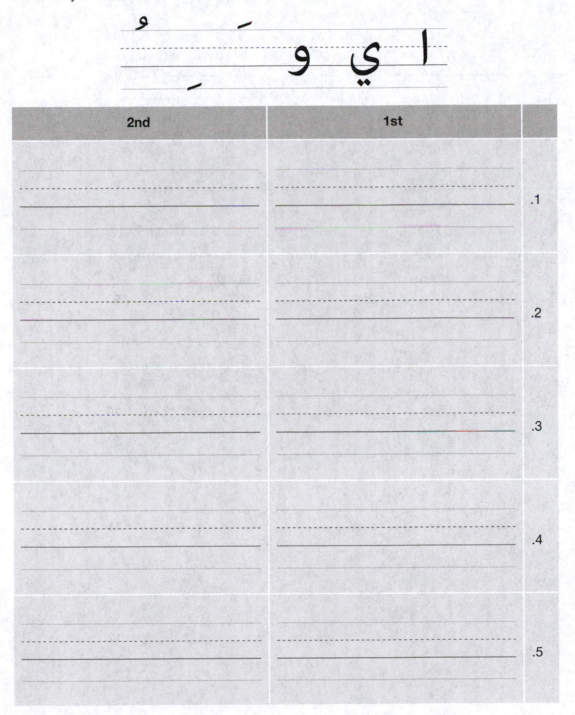

2nd	1st	
		.1
		.2
		.3
		.4
		.5

2nd	1st	
		.6
		.7
		.8
		.9
		.10
		.11
		.12

2nd	1st	
		.13
		.14
		.15

Activity 35 Dictation practice: short vowels

نشاط ٣٥   تدريب علي الإملاء: الحركات

Listen to the words and write them in Arabic letters. This time, be sure to write all of the short vowels.

_____ .1

_____ .2

_____ .3

_____ .4

_____ .5

_____ .6

_____ .7

_____ .8

You have learned that the short vowels in Arabic must always "sit" on top of or below a letter. What happens when we want to write the short vowel sound ◌َ (a) at the beginning of a word?

 The same rule applies: the short vowel must still sit on top of a letter. The *fatHa* (a) sits above the letter ا and another symbol called "*hamza*." The *hamza* represents a sudden burst of air commonly pronounced at the start of words beginning with a vowel, like in *apple* and *as*. English speakers are not used to thinking of this as a distinct, meaningful sound, but that is how Arabic treats it. (The *hamza* also can appear in the middle of words—think of the exclamation *uh-oh*—and you will learn more about this in Part Seven.)

Name: *alif-hamza* (As you can see, this is not its own letter but a combination of symbols.)

Sound: This combination of ألف (*alif*) + فتحة (*fatHa*) + همزة (*hamza*) makes the exact same sound as the short vowel *fatHa* (a), despite the *alif* shape. Listen to the following words and practice saying them aloud:

أَمر أَكثَر أَقول أَنا

Shape: Because this combination appears only at the beginning of the word and *alif* is an anti-social letter, it takes only one shape. Write the *alif*, then the *hamza* above it, then the *fatHa* on top.

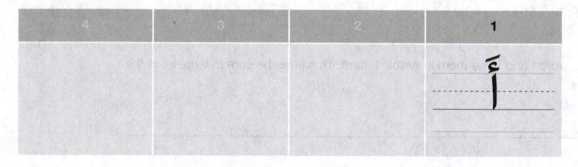

4	3	2	1
			أَ

 Other short vowels can also sit on *alif-hamza* at the beginning of the word, and you will learn more about these combinations later; we are teaching you *alif-hamza* now because it is part of many common words.

Activity 36 Practice writing *fatHa* on *alif-hamza*

نشاط ٣٦ تدريب على كتابة الفتحة على الهمزة والألف

Practice writing أَ across one line. Say the sound aloud as you write it.

أَ

What does this combination remind you of? How will you help yourself remember its sound? Draw a picture or write some notes here:

Activity 37 Practice reading *fatHa* on *alif-hamza*	نشاط ٣٧ تدريب على قراءة الفتحة على الهمزة والألف

Practice reading these words with أَ in them aloud. Remember to make your pronunciation of this combination short, like you would when pronouncing a short vowel.

أَتَت   أَثوب   أَبي   أَثاث   أَب

Activity 38 Dictation practice: *fatHa* on *alif-hamza*	نشاط ٣٨ تدريب على الإملاء: فتحة وهمزة على الألف 🎧

Listen to the dictated words and write them down as precisely as you can in Arabic letters. Be sure to write the short vowels.

1. _____

2. _____

3. _____

4. _____

5. _____

REVIEW   المراجعة

Congratulations! You have a solid start on your journey to Arabic proficiency. If you feel you are struggling with any concepts, letters, or shapes from this chapter, take some time to review them or ask your teacher for help. A strong foundation from the beginning will help you master the remaining letters. Here are some activities to help you review.

Activity 39 Letter connection practice   نشاط ٣٩ تدريب على ربط الحروف

Connect the letters as appropriate to form words. Then listen to the recording of the words and add the short vowels that you hear.

١. أ + ب + ا = _____

٢. ت + و + ب + ث = _____

٣. ب + و + ت + أ = _____

٤. ب + ا + ب + ت = _____

٥. ي + ب + و + ث + ت = _____

٦. ت + ي + ت + ب + ت = _____

Activity 40 Practice reading handwriting   نشاط ٤٠ تدريب على قراءة خط اليد

An important part of learning to read Arabic is recognizing how letters' appearances vary in print versus handwriting. Practice reading these handwritten words out loud:

نَتُب   ثابت   ثُبوت   تَوت   تَثْبيت   ثِياب

Activity 41 Dictation practice

نشاط ٤١   تدريب على الإملاء

Listen to the dictated words and write them down as precisely as you can in Arabic letters. Be sure to write the short vowels.

_____ .1

_____ .2

_____ .3

_____ .4

_____ .5

_____ .6

PART TWO

الجزء الثاني

أهداف الجزء الثاني

PART TWO GOALS

By the end of this section, you should be able to do the following:

- Read, write, pronounce, and connect the consonants: ل م ن هـ
- Read, write, and pronounce *waaw* and *yaa'* as consonants
- Read, write, and pronounce Arabic's diphthongs
- Read, write, and understand the symbol *sukuun*: ـْ

REVIEW: HOW TO CONNECT ARABIC LETTERS

للمراجعة: كيفية ربط الحروف العربية

Remember that every Arabic letter has **four different shapes**, used depending on where the letter is in a word and what kind of letter comes before it. Use this chart as a reference for how to use the different shapes of each letter that you learn in this chapter.

4	3	2	1
A shape for when the letter is at the **end** of a word **after an anti-social letter** *or* when the shape is written **by itself**, as in an alphabet poster	A shape for when the letter is at the **end** of a word **after a social letter**	A shape for when the letter is in the **middle** of a word **after a social letter**	A shape for when the letter is at the **beginning** of a word *or* when the letter is in the **middle** of a word **after an anti-social letter**

Remember that even though the shapes of one letter look different, they all represent the same sound.

Letter name: لام (*laam*)

Sound: The letter *laam* sounds similar to an *l* in English when that *l* is pronounced with the tip of your tongue touching your teeth, as in *lemon* (this is called the "light *l*" sound). What other English words can you think of that have a light *l* sound? English also has another *l* sound, called the "dark *l*," which you pronounce with your tongue drawn back into your mouth, not touching your teeth, as in *toll* and *fall*. The dark *l* sound is rarely used in Arabic. Focusing on using the light *l* sound will improve your Arabic pronunciation.

Listen to *laam* in the following words and repeat them aloud:

قَبَلَ   بَلَد   بال   لَيسَ

Social/antisocial: This letter is social.

Shapes: In some ways this shape is similar to *alif*, but it is a social letter and has a distinctive final shape that drops below the line.

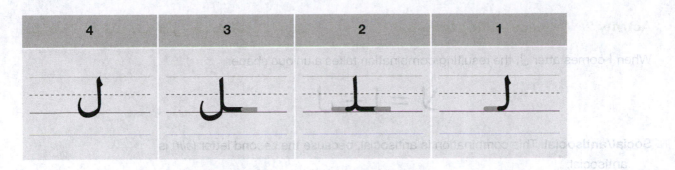

4	3	2	1
ل	ـل	ـلـ	لـ

Activity 1   Practice writing *laam*

نشاط ١   تدريب على كتابة اللام

Practice writing each form of ل as many times as you can across one line. Say the sound aloud as you write it.

ل

ـل

ـلـ

لـ

What does this letter's appearance remind you of? How will you help yourself remember its sound? Draw a picture or write some notes here:

Activity 2　Practice writing *laam-alif*　　نشاط ٢　تدريب على كتابة اللام والألف

When ‍ا comes after ل, the resulting combination takes a unique shape:

$$ لا = ا + ل $$

Social/antisocial: This combination is antisocial, because the second letter (*alif*) is antisocial.

Shapes: The shapes for *laam-alif* appear differently in printed text and in handwriting. Both forms are presented here.

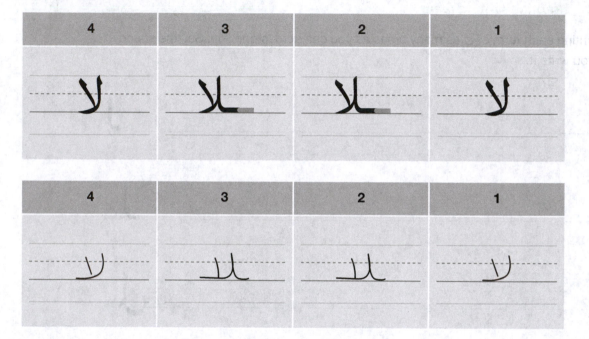

This combination appears within many words, but it is also a word by itself, meaning "no." Practice writing the forms of *laam-alif* across one line. Say this word aloud as you write it.

Activity 3 Reading practice: Where are the letters? (*alif* and *laam*)

نشاط ٣ تدريب على القراءة: أين الحروف؟ (الألف واللام)

Scan these lines from the poem "Don't Cry, Laila" by the classical Arab poet Abu Nuwas, and circle each instance you see of ا and ل. At the beginning and middle of words, these letters look almost the same—how will you be able to tell them apart?

واشْرَب على الوَرْدِ من حمراء كالوَرْدِ   لا تَبْكِ ليلى ولا تطْرَبْ إلى هندِ

من كفِّ جاريةٍ ممشوقةِ القَدِّ   فالخمرُ ياقوتةٌ والكأسُ لؤلؤةٌ

شيءٌ خُصصتُ به مِن دونِهم وحدي   لي نشوتانِ وللندمانِ واحدةٌ

How many do you see of each? ا: _____ ل: _____

Activity 4 Letter connection practice: *laam*

نشاط ٤ تدريب على ربط الحروف: اللام

Connect the letters as appropriate to form words.

1. ي + ل + ي = _____
2. ث + ي + ل = _____
3. ب + ا + ل = _____
4. أ + و + ل + ا + ث = _____
5. ث + ي + و + ل + ت = _____

Activity 5   Practice writing *alif-laam*   تدريب على كتابة الألف-لام   ٥ نشاط

Remember that the opposite combination of ا followed by ل does not connect in any special way; in fact, they do not connect to each other in this order at all. Why not?

    This is the Arabic word for "the." One important thing to remember is that "the" in Arabic is not a separate word: it is *always* written as part of the word that comes next in the sentence. Practice writing the combination *alif-laam* across one line, with the *laam* in beginning form. Say this combination aloud as you write it.

الـ

    Now, practice writing two different words with الـ connected to them, pronouncing the combination as you write. The first word means "the door" and the second word means "the berries," but you do not need to memorize these words right now; just practice writing them and saying them aloud.

الباب

التوت

Activity 6   Practice reading *laam*   تدريب على قراءة اللام   ٦ نشاط

Practice reading these words out loud, making your pronunciation of long vowels last at least twice as long as that of short vowels.

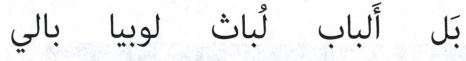

بالي   لوبيا   لُباث   أَلباب   بَل

Activity 7   Dictation practice: *laam*   تدريب على الإملاء: اللام   ٧ نشاط

Listen to the dictation words and write them down as precisely as you can in Arabic letters. Be sure to write the short vowels.

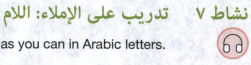

١. _____

٢. _____

_____ 3.

_____ 4.

_____ 5.

_____ 6.

_____ 7.

_____ 8.

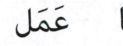

Letter name: ميم (*miim*)

Sound: *miim* sounds like the English letter *m*. Listen to *miim* in the following words and repeat them:

كَلام   مُهِمّ   عَمَل   ما

Social/antisocial: This letter is social.

Shapes: The special feature of this letter is a small circle.

4	3	2	1
م	مم	ـمـ	مـ

In the handwriting style shown below, the small circles of *miim* are not filled in, but some handwriting styles fill in the circular part completely. Work with your teacher to decide which style you will practice but learn to recognize all of these forms.

4	3	2	1
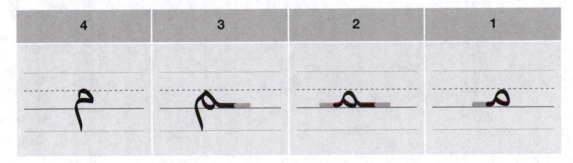			

نشاط ٨   تدريب على كتابة الميم **Activity 8   Practice writing** *miim*

Practice writing each form of م as many times as you can across one line. Say the sound aloud as you write it.

What does this letter's appearance remind you of? How will you help yourself remember its sound? Draw a picture or write some notes here:

Activity 9   Practice writing *laam* **and** *miim*   تدريب على كتابة اللام والميم   ٩ نشاط

The letter م has one more special shape to learn about. When you see the combination of ل (in beginning form) and then م directly after it, you will notice that the combination can look a little different than you expect in some fonts.

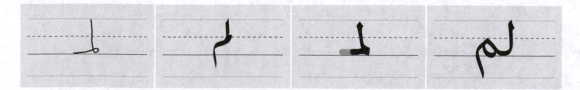

Practice writing the word المال ("the money") across one line, copying the way it looks in different fonts and in handwriting:

المال

المال

المال

المال

Activity 10 Letter connection practice:
miim

نشاط ١٠   تدريب على ربط الحروف: الميم

Connect the letters as appropriate to form words.

١. م + و + ت = _____

٢. أ + ي + ا + م = _____

٣. م + ي + ت + ي = _____

٤. م + و + ل + ي = _____

٥. م + و + م + ل + م = _____

Activity 11 Practice reading *miim*

نشاط ١١   تدريب على قراءة الميم

Practice reading these words out loud, making your pronunciation of long vowels last at least twice as long as that of short vowels.

لِثام   مَثاث   مَبيت   أَلَم   ماما

Activity 12 Dictation practice: *miim*   نشاط ١٢   تدريب على الإملاء: الميم

Listen to the dictation words and write them down as precise as you can in Arabic letters.
Be sure to write the short vowels.

_____ .1

_____ .2

_____ .3

_____ .4

_____ .5

_____ .6

_____ .7

_____ .8

Letter name: نون (*nuun*)

Sound: *nuun* sounds like the English letter *n*. Listen to *nuun* in the following words and
  repeat them:

كانَ   مِن   اِثنَين   ناس

Social/antisocial: This letter is social.

Shapes: Look carefully at the shapes. How is *nuun* similar to and different from these
  letters: ب ت ث ي؟

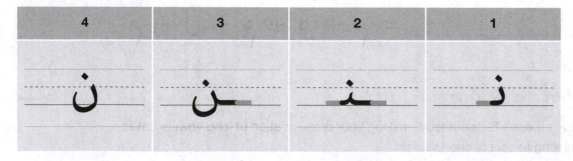

4	3	2	1
ن	ـن	ـنـ	نـ

Activity 13 Practice writing *nuun*   نشاط ١٣   تدريب على كتابة النون

Practice writing each form of ن as many times as you can across one line. Say the sound aloud as you write it.

ـنـ

ـنـ

ـن

ن

What does this letter's appearance remind you of? How will you help yourself remember its sound? Draw a picture or write some notes here:

Activity 14 Letter connection practice: نشاط ١٤   تدريب على ربط الحروف:
**   *nuun***   النون

Connect the letters as appropriate to form words.

١. م + ن = ــــــــــــــــــــــــ

٢. ب + ي + ا + ن = ــــــــــــــــــــــــ

٣. ا + ل + ي + و + ن + ا + ن = _____

٤. ب + ي + ن + م + ا = _____

٥. ن + ي + ا + ت = _____

| Activity 15 Practice writing *nuun* in pronouns | نشاط ١٥   تدريب على كتابة النون في الضمائر |

This letter appears in three very common words that you have already learned how to say: the word for "I," the word for "you" (masculine), and the word for "you" (feminine). Practice writing each across one line, saying them as you write them:

أَنا

أَنتَ

أَنتِ

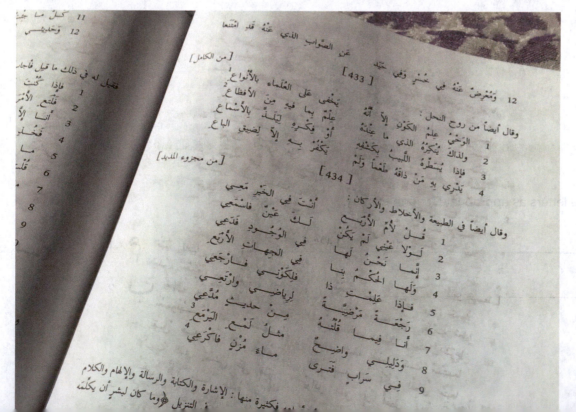

Activity 16 Practice reading *nuun*   تدريب على قراءة النون   نشاط ١٦

Practicing reading these words out loud. Keep practicing the long and short vowels, making your pronunciation of long vowels last at least twice as long as that of short vowels.
Some of these words are place names—can you guess their meaning?

أَبيت   أَلمانيا   أَثينا   بَنات   لُبنان

Activity 17 Dictation practice: *nuun*   تدريب على الإملاء: النون   نشاط ١٧

Listen to the dictation words and write them down as precisely as you can in Arabic letters.
Be sure to write the short vowels.

_____ .1

_____ .2

_____ .3

_____ .4

_____ .5

_____ .6

_____ .7

_____ .8

Letter name: هاء (*haa'*)

Sound: *haa'* sounds like the English letter *h*. This sound is more likely to come in the middle and at the end of words in Arabic than in English. Listen to *haa'* in the following words and repeat them:

أَكثَرُهُ   طِفلُهُ   مِثلَها   هَل

Social/antisocial: This letter is social.

Shapes: The four shapes of *haa'* vary significantly. Notice that when the letter is written by itself in alphabet lists, people usually use the beginning form (see the letter in the circle on the previous page).

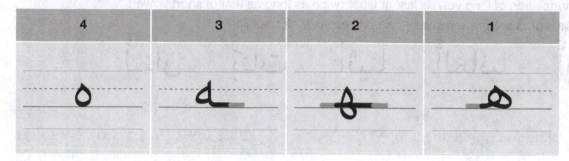

The middle form of *haa'* can vary between different handwriting styles, usually taking one of two different shapes:

Work with your teacher to decide which style you will practice, but learn to recognize all of these forms.

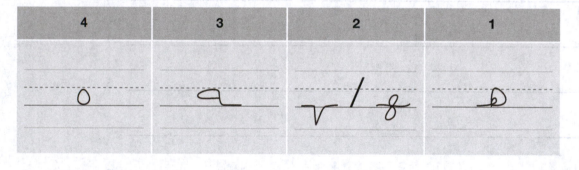

Activity 18 Practice writing *haa'*   نشاط ١٨ تدريب على كتابة الهاء

Practice writing each form of ﻫ as many times as you can across one line. Say the sound aloud as you write it.

ــه

ه

You can practice three of هـ's shapes by writing out the sound of laughter in Arabic. This is not an official word, but it is used in Arabic like "hahaha" in English.

ههههه

What does this letter's appearance remind you of? How will you help yourself remember its sound? Draw a picture or write some notes here:

نشاط ١٩   تدريب على القراءة: أين الحروف؟ (الميم والهاء)
Activity 19   Reading practice: Where are the letters? (*miim* and *haa'*)

Scan these lines from the poem "Al-Mutanabbi to Sayf al-Dawla" by the classical Arab poet al-Mutanabbi, and circle each instance you see of م and هـ. These lines are all from the same poem, but they do not necessarily come consecutively in the original.

وتأتي على قدر الكرام المكارم	على قدر أهل العزم تأتي العزائم
وقد عجزت عنه الجيوش الخضارم	يكلّف سيف الدولة الجيش همَّه
فلما دنا منها سقتها الجماجم	سقتْها الغمامُ الغُرُّ قبل نزوله
ثيابُهم من مثلها وعمائم	إذا برقوا لم تُعرَف البيضُ منهم

How many do you see of each? م: _____ هـ: _____

Activity 20 Letter connection practice: *haa'*   نشاط ٢٠   تدريب على ربط الحروف: الهاء

Connect the letters as appropriate to form words.

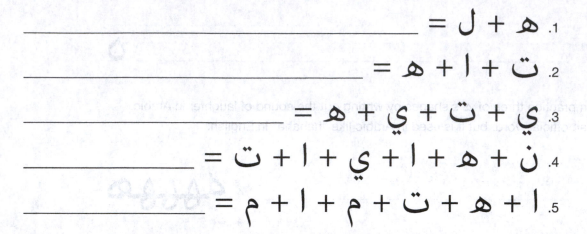

١. هـ + ل = ـ_____

٢. هـ + ا + ت = _____

٣. هـ + ي + ت + ي = _____

٤. ت + ا + ي + هـ + ن = _____

٥. م + ا + ت + م + ا + هـ = _____

Activity 21 Practice reading *haa'*   نشاط ٢١   تدريب على قراءة الهاء

Practice reading these words out loud. Keep practicing the long and short vowels, making
your pronunciation of long vowels last at least twice as long as that of short vowels.

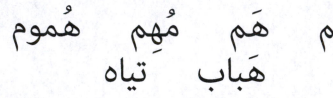

هُمْ   هَمَ   مُهِمّ   هُموم
هَباب   تياه

Activity 22 Dictation practice: *haa'*   نشاط ٢٢   تدريب على الإملاء: الهاء

Listen to the dictation words and write them down as precisely as you can in Arabic letters.
Be sure to write the short vowels.

_____.١

_____.٢

_____.٣

_____.٤

_____.٥

.6 _____

.7 _____

.8 _____

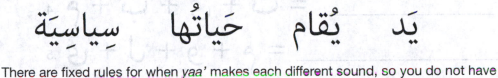

This is the same letter *yaa'* you learned in Part One, with the same name and the same shapes. Now, you will learn about another sound that this letter makes.

Sound: You have already learned that *yaa'* makes a long vowel *ii* sound as in *eel*. *yaa'* can also make the sound of a consonant, which sounds just like the English letter *y*. Listen to *yaa'* as a consonant in the following words and repeat them aloud:

سِياسِيَة   حَياتُها   يُقام   يَد

There are fixed rules for when *yaa'* makes each different sound, so you do not have to guess. In general, *yaa'* makes a consonant sound when it appears before or after a long or short vowel. Here is an overview of what you know about the different sounds that *yaa'* makes:

Sound	When it makes this sound	Examples
ii as in *eel*	Between two consonants At the end of a word (unless it is next to another vowel)	تَبتيت، مالي
y as in *you*	Next to a vowel, long or short At the beginning of a word	يَنمو، بُيوت

Activity 23 Letter connection practice: *yaa'* (as a consonant)

نشاط ٢٣   تدريب على ربط الحروف: الياء (حرف ساكن)

Connect the letters as appropriate to form words. Then listen to the recording of the words and add the short vowels that you hear. Say the words after the recording and pay attention to both kinds of *yaa'*.

$$\text{١. } \text{م} + \text{ي} + \text{ت} + \text{ي} = \underline{\hspace{6cm}}$$

$$\text{٢. } \text{ن} + \text{و} + \text{م} + \text{ي} + \text{ل} = \underline{\hspace{5cm}}$$

$$\text{٣. } \text{ي} + \text{ن} + \text{ا} + \text{ن} + \text{و} + \text{ي} = \underline{\hspace{4cm}}$$

$$\text{٤. } \text{ت} + \text{ي} + \text{ب} + \text{م} = \underline{\hspace{5cm}}$$

$$\text{٥. } \text{م} + \text{و} + \text{ل} + \text{ي} = \underline{\hspace{6cm}}$$

Activity 24 Practice reading *yaa'* (as a consonant)

نشاط ٢٤   تدريب قراءة الياء (حرف ساكن)

Read each of the following words out loud, focusing on pronouncing ي correctly as either *ii* or *y*.

بَيان   يَمين   اليَمَن   ميم   يَلي

Activity 25 Dictation practice: *yaa'* (as a consonant)

نشاط ٢٥   تدريب على الإملاء: الياء (حرف ساكن)

Listen to the dictation words and write them down as precisely as you can in Arabic letters. Be sure to write the short vowels.

_____ .١

_____ .٢

_____ .٣

_____ .٤

_____ .٥

_____ 6.

_____ 7.

_____ 8.

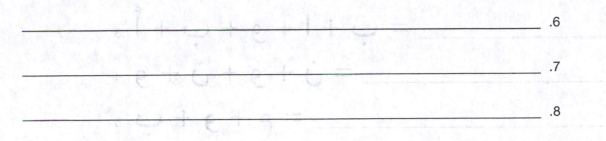

This is the same letter *waaw* you learned in Part One, with the same name and the same shapes. Now you will learn about another sound that this letter makes.

Sound: You have already learned that *waaw* makes a long vowel *uu* sound as in *spook*. *waaw* can also make the sound of a consonant, which sounds just like the English letter *w*. Listen to *waaw* as a consonant in the following words and repeat them aloud:

نَحوَ   دُوَل   صُوَر   واجِب

Like *yaa'*, there are fixed rules for when *waaw* makes each different sound. In general, *waaw* makes a consonant sound when it appears before or after a long or short vowel. Here is an overview of what you know about the different sounds that *waaw* makes:

Sound	When it makes this sound	Examples
uu as in *spook*	Between two consonants At the end of a word (unless it is next to a vowel)	مَلموم، تَنمو
w as in *well*	Next to a vowel, long or short At the beginning of a word	والي، أموال

Activity 26 Letter connection practice:
**   waaw (as a consonant)**

نشاط ٢٦   تدريب على ربط الحروف: الواو
(حرف ساكن)

Connect the letters as appropriate to form words. Then listen to the recording of the words and add the short vowels that you hear. Say the words after the recording and pay attention to both kinds of *waaw*.

1. ن + و + ن = _____

2. و + ه + ا + ب + ي = _____

$$ \underline{\hspace{6cm}} = ب + ا + و + ب + أ ._3 $$
$$ \underline{\hspace{6cm}} = ن + و + ن + و ._4 $$
$$ \underline{\hspace{6cm}} = م + و + ب ._5 $$

Activity 27 Practice reading *waaw*   نشاط ٢٧   تدريب على قراءة الواو
         (as a consonant)   (حرف ساكن)

Read each of the following words out loud, focusing on pronouncing و correctly as either *w* or *uu*.

ألواث   ليمون   يَموت

أموال   يَلوم

Activity 28 Practice writing *waaw* in   نشاط ٢٨   تدريب على كتابة الواو في
         words   الكلمات

One of the most common words in Arabic features the letter و as a consonant:

وَ   and

Like الـ ("the"), the word وَ ("and") is written directly adjacent to the following word in the sentence, with no space between them.

Practice writing the phase وَأَنتَ؟ ("And you?") across this line, speaking it aloud each time you write it. Remember not to put a space after و.

وَأَنتَ؟

The letters و and ي also appear as consonants in two extremely important Arabic words: the pronouns meaning "he" and "she." Practice writing them each across one line, saying them out loud as you do so.

هُوَ

هِـيَ

Activity 29 Dictation practice: *waaw*
(as a consonant)

نشاط ٢٩   تدريب على الإملاء: الواو
(حرف ساكن)

Listen to the dictation words and write them down as precisely as you can in Arabic letters.
Be sure to write the short vowels.

_____ .1

_____ .2

_____ .3

_____ .4

_____ .5

_____ .6

_____ .7

_____ .8

Arabic has two diphthongs. These are sounds formed by the combination of two of Arabic's vowel sounds in the same syllable. The first diphthong we will learn is the combination of *fatHa* and *yaa'*. This combination makes a sound we will write as "*ay*." This combination may vary a little from word to word but sounds similar to the vowel sound in *buy* or *say*. Listen to this diphthong in the following words and repeat them aloud:

خَير   عَين   حَيثُ   بَينَ

In many dialects, the sound of this combination shifts slightly. To hear this sound in dialect, try pronouncing the word *hay* without moving your tongue at all; the vowel sound you will make is very similar to the sound of *ay* in dialect.

Here is an overview of the three sounds that *yaa'* makes:

Sound	When it makes this sound	Examples
ii as in *eel*	Between two consonants At the end of a word (unless it is next to a vowel)	تَبتيت، مالي
y as in *you*	Next to a vowel, long or short At the beginning of a word	يَنمو، بُيوت
ay as in *buy* or *say*	After a *fatHa*	هَيل، أَينَ

Activity 30 Listening practice: *ay*   نشاط ٣٠   تدريب على الاستماع: يَ

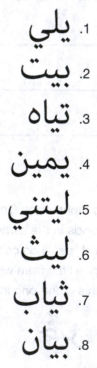

Listen to the following words with ي in them. Add the short vowels you hear. If ي is part of a diphthong, be sure to add a *fatHa* to the previous letter.

١. يلي

٢. بيت

٣. تياه

٤. يمين

٥. ليتني

٦. ليث

٧. ثياب

٨. بيان

Activity 31 Reading practice: *ay*   نشاط ٣١ تدريب على القراءة: ـَي

Read the following fully voweled words out loud, then rewrite them in the appropriate box below.

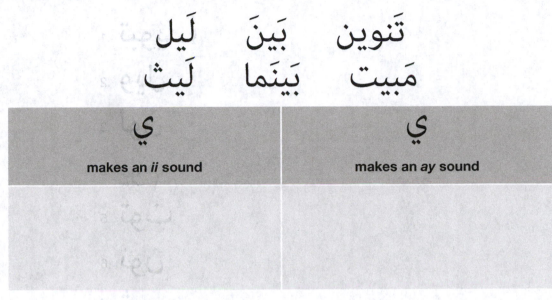

تَنوين بَيْنَ لَيْل
مَبيت بَيْنَما لَيْث

ي	ي
makes an *ii* sound	makes an *ay* sound

The other diphthong in Arabic is the combination of *fatHa* and *waaw*. This combination makes a sound we will write as "*aw*," found in English words like *chow*, *out*, and *now*. Listen to this diphthong in the following words and repeat them aloud:

نَوعاً مَوقِف صَوت يَوم

In many dialects, this combination is pronounced more like *o* as in *go*. To make this sound in Arabic, try pronouncing the word *go* without moving your lips at all.

Here is an overview of the three sounds that *waaw* makes:

Sound	When it makes this sound	Examples
uu as in *spook*	Between two consonants At the end of a word (unless it is next to a vowel)	مَلموم، تَنمو
w as in *well*	Next to a vowel, long or short At the beginning of a word	والي، أَموال
aw as in *chow*	After a *fatHa*	نَوم، لَو

Activity 32 Listening practice: *aw*   نشاط ٣٢ تدريب على الاستماع: ـَو

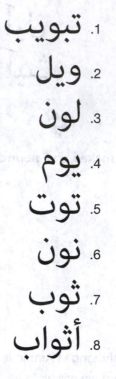

Listen to the following words with و in them. Add the short vowels you hear. If و is part of a diphthong, be sure add a *fatHa* to the previous letter.

١. تبويب

٢. ويل

٣. لون

٤. يوم

٥. توت

٦. نون

٧. ثوب

٨. أثواب

Activity 33 Reading practice: *aw*   نشاط ٣٣ تدريب على القراءة: ـَو

Read the following fully voweled words out loud, then rewrite them in the appropriate box below.

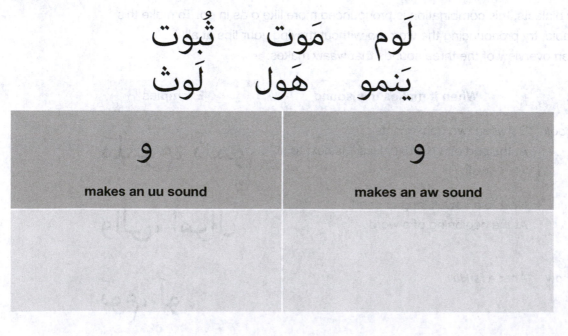

لَوم   مَوت   ثُبوت

يَنمو   هَول   لَوث

و	و
makes an uu sound	**makes an aw sound**

How will you help yourself remember the diphthongs in Arabic? Draw a picture or write some notes here:

Like the short vowels, this shape is one of the non-letter symbols that are part of the Arabic writing system.

Name: سُكون (*sukuun*)

Shape: *sukuun* is an optional symbol that is written above letters. Its shape is simply a small circle.

Sound: *sukuun* has no sound. Instead, when it sits on a letter it tells a reader that there is no long or short vowel after that letter. It represents the absence of a vowel. The word "*sukuun*" itself means "silence" or "tranquility." When *sukuun* is written above *yaa'* or *waaw* (ـيْ or ـوْ), it signals that these letters are to be pronounced as consonants (*y* or *w*) or as diphthongs (*ay* or *aw*).

Listen to the following words and practice reading them aloud to observe how *sukuun* is used:

بَيْت ثَوْب ثُلْثان مِثْلي

You may wonder why Arabic needs such a shape. Why bother writing a "silent" symbol on something? The *sukuun* symbol was invented to help readers pronounce words correctly in the Qur'an, where reading each letter and word accurately is considered extremely important. Similarly, writers today use the *sukuun* symbol to help readers distinguish between words that have different meanings but look the same if written without this symbol. In such cases, a *sukuun* may be written even when short vowels elsewhere in the word are not written:

I began	بدأتُ
She began	بدأتْ

For a reader, seeing a *sukuun* on بدأتْ makes clear that this word means "she began," rather than "I began." Except for purposes like this, *sukuun* is rarely written in most kinds of texts.

In most cases, you will not need to write *sukuun*. However, it will be useful to you when reading or writing words for learning and memorization, so that you can be sure of the correct pronunciation.

Activity 34　Listening practice: *sukuun*　　　　نشاط ٣٤　تدريب على الاستماع: السكون

Listen to the following words and phrases and write in the vowels you hear. When you do not hear a short vowel after a consonant, write *sukuun* instead.

　　You should recognize the meaning of some, but not all, of these words and phrases. Which sound familiar? What do they mean?

١. ليالي

٢. أنا من

٣. هو

٤. تبويب

٥. هي

٦. نوم

٧. ينتمي

٨. تنمو

٩. أنت

١٠. من أين؟

١١. تثبيت

١٢. هلال

١٣. من وين؟

١٤. أنت

١٥. تهتم

How will you help yourself remember this symbol and its position? Draw a picture or write some notes here:

REVIEW   المراجعة

Congratulations on your progress with the Arabic alphabet! In this section, there are some practice activities to help you review what you have learned so far. Before starting, look over the letters covered in Part One and Part Two and review the ones that are most difficult for you. As you work through the activities, pay attention to which letters and sounds you make mistakes with. If you feel you are struggling with certain letters or shapes from this chapter, take some time to review them or ask your teacher for help.

Activity 35 Reading and listening practice نشاط ٣٥ تدريب على القراءة والاستماع

First, read each of the following words aloud. Check your pronunciation with a classmate. Second, listen to the ten words on the recording: you will hear *one* of each pair in the list. Circle the one you hear. Check your answers when you are done, and practice reading each word aloud again.

1. لام   أَلَم

2. ثَبات   ثابِت

3. نَمال   نَمْل

4. هُم   هَم

5. بات   بَيت

6. اِثْنَين   اِثْنان

7. واهِب   وَهاب

8. أَيتام   يَتيم

9. اِهْتِمام   أَهْتَم

10. بال   بِلا

Activity 36 Letter connection practice   نشاط ٣٦   تدريب على ربط الحروف   🎧

Connect the letters as appropriate to form words. Then listen to the recording of the words and add the short vowels that you hear.

.1   هـ + ي =   _____

.2   ي + و + م =   _____

.3   ل + ث + م =   _____

.4   م + ي + ا + هـ =   _____

.5   ب + و + ل + ل =   _____

.6   هـ + ل + ا + ل =   _____

.7   ت + ب + و + ي + ب =   _____

.8   م + هـ + و + ا + أ =   _____

Activity 37 Practice reading handwriting   نشاط ٣٧   تدريب على قراءة خط اليد

Practice reading these handwritten words out loud:

مُهِمَّات   هَل   أَهَمّ   تاه

Activity 38 Dictation practice   نشاط ٣٨   تدريب على الإملاء   🎧

Listen to the dictation words and write them down as precisely as you can in Arabic letters. Be sure to write the short vowels.

1. _____

2. _____

3. _____

.4 _____

.5 _____

.6 _____

.7 _____

.8 _____

.9 _____

.10 _____

PART THREE

الجزء الثالث

أهداف الجزء الثالث

PART THREE GOALS

By the end of this section, you should be able to do the following:

- Read, write, pronounce, and connect the consonants: غ ع خ ح ج
- Review your skills with the letters that you have learned in previous parts

REVIEW: HOW TO CONNECT ARABIC LETTERS

للمراجعة: كيفية ربط الحروف العربية

Remember that every Arabic letter has **four different shapes**, used depending on where the letter is in a word and what kind of letter comes before it. Use this chart as a reference for how to use the different shapes of each letter.

4	3	2	1
A shape for when the letter is at the **end** of a word **after an anti-social letter** *or* when the shape is written **by itself**, as in an alphabet poster	A shape for when the letter is at the **end** of a word **after a social letter**	A shape for when the letter is in the **middle** of a word **after a social letter**	A shape for when the letter is at the **begin-ning** of a word *or* when the letter is in the **middle** of a word **after an anti-social letter**

Remember that even though the shapes of one letter look different, they all represent the same sound.

Letter name: جيم (*jiim*)

Sound: This letter is pronounced slightly different in different parts of the Arab world: it can sound like the *g* in *good*, the *g* in *beige*, or the *j* in *justice*. Try pronouncing the name of the letter (جيم) with each of the three different sounds.

    In classical Arabic, the letter ج sounds like the *j* in *justice*, which is the pronunciation we will practice now. Listen to how your teacher and other Arabic speakers you meet say this letter and imitate them. Listen to *jiim* in the following words and repeat them aloud:

 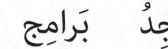

تاج   بَرامِج   يَجِدُ   جَديد

Social/antisocial: This letter is social.

Shapes: Look at the different shapes for *jiim* and identify the distinguishing features.

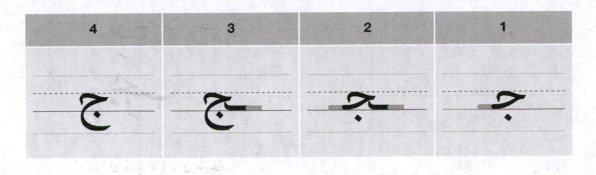

نشاط ١   تدريب على كتابة الجيم   **Activity 1   Practice writing** *jiim*

Practice writing each form of ج as many times as you can across one line. Say the sound aloud as you write it.

In some print and handwriting styles, social letters that come before ج are written above the line so that the combination can be written without lifting one's pencil from the paper. Practice writing the following words that show this, so that you can recognize this kind of combination.

نُ + ج + و + م = نُجوم

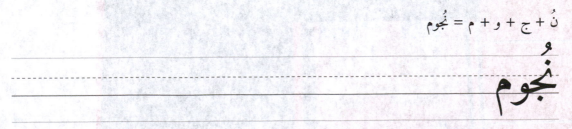

يَ + جِ + ب = يَجِب

يَجِب

لِ + جِ + ا + ن = لِجان

لِجان

What does this letter's appearance remind you of? How will you help yourself remember its sound? Draw a picture or write some notes here:

Activity 2   **Letter connection practice:**   نشاط ٢   تدريب على ربط الحروف:
jiim   الجيم

Connect the letters as appropriate to form words. Then listen to the recording of the words
and add the short vowels that you hear.

١. ج + ا + ت = _____

٢. م + و + ج + ن = _____

٣. و + ه + ج + و = _____

٤. ج + و + ن + ب = _____

٥. أ + ج + ا + ن + ب = _____

٦. م + ج + ا + ل + ا + ت = _____

Activity 3   **Practice reading** *jiim*   نشاط ٣   تدريب على قراءة الجيم

Practice reading these words containing ج out loud.

يُجيب   جَميل   وَجَبَ

أَجابَت   أَجْلِهِ   جانِب

Activity 4   **Dictation practice:** *jiim*   نشاط ٤   تدريب على الإملاء: الجيم

Listen to the dictation words and write them down as precisely as you can in Arabic letters.
Write all of the short vowels.

١. _____

٢. _____

٣. _____

٤. _____

_____ .5

_____ .6

_____ .7

_____ .8

Letter name: حاء (*Haa'*)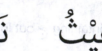

Sound: This letter sounds very similar to ـه (*haa'*) for many English speakers; if your native language is not English, this letter may be easier for you. While ـه (*haa'*) sounds very similar to an English *h*, ح (*Haa'*) is a breathy sound that comes from tightening the flow of air in the throat. When writing Arabic words in English letters in this book, capital "*H*" represents ح.

ح (*Haa'*) is the sound you make fogging up a mirror with your breath

ه (*haa'*) is in the onomatopoeia for laughter in English and Arabic

Listen to *Haa'* in the following words and repeat them aloud.

راح   أَصْبَحَ   نَحْنُ   حَيْثُ

Social/antisocial: This letter is social.

Shapes: The shapes for *Haa'* are the same as those for *jiim* but without any dot.

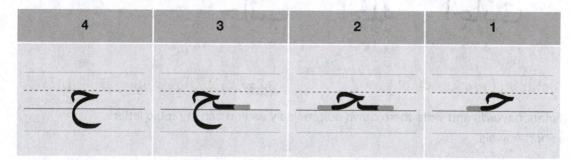

4	3	2	1
ح	ح	ح	ح

Activity 5   Practice writing *Haa'*

Practice writing each form of ح as many times as you can across one line. Say the sound aloud as you write it.

ح

حـ

ـحـ

ـح

As with ج, social letters that come before ح are sometimes written above the line. Practice writing the following words that show this, so that you can recognize this kind of combination.

نَ + حْ + نُ = نَحْنُ

نَحْنُ

مَ + حْ + م + و + د = مَحْمود

مَحْمود

لُ + حْ + و + م = لُحُوم

لُحُوم

What does this letter's appearance remind you of? How will you help yourself remember its sound? Draw a picture or write some notes here:

Activity 6   Letter connection practice: *Haa'*

تدريب على ربط الحروف: الحاء   نشاط ٦

Connect the following letters—or not, depending on whether they are social or antisocial—to form Arabic words. Next, listen to the recording of the words and add the short vowels.

_____ = ح + و + ل .1

_____ = ب + ح + و + ث .2

_____ = ح + ا + ل + ي .3

_____ = ح + ب + ي + ب .4

_____ = ح + ن + ج + ا + ح .5

_____ = ا + ح + ت + ل + ا + ل .6

Activity 7   Listening practice: *Haa'* vs. *haa'*

تدريب على الاستماع: الحاء مقابل الهاء   نشاط ٧

Practice hearing and recognizing the difference between the letters ح and ـه.

You will hear a list of words. For each one, mark an X in the column that represents the sound you heard in that word. For example, if you hear the word الحمد and you recognize the sound as a ح, put an X in the ح column. You will hear some letters that you do not know how to write yet, but focus on the difference between ح and ـه.

	ح	هـ
.1		
.2		
.3		
.4		
.5		
.6		
.7		
.8		
.9		
.10		

Activity 8   Practice reading *Haa'*   تدريب على قراءة الحاء   نشاط ٨

Practice reading these words containing ح and ـهـ out loud. Focus on enunciating the difference between these two letters clearly.

حُب   هَم   حَج

مالح   نِهايات   لَحْم

Activity 9   Dictation practice: *Haa'*   تدريب على الإملاء: الحاء   نشاط ٩

Listen to the dictation words and write them down as precisely as you can in Arabic letters. Some of these words may have ـهـ instead of ح, so listen carefully!

.1 _____

.2 _____

.3 _____

_____ .4

_____ .5

_____ .6

_____ .7

_____ .8

_____ .9

_____ .10

Letter name: خاء (*khaa'*)

Sound: The خ sound is made deep in the throat and is not found in many English words. Listen to *khaa'* in the following words and repeat them aloud.

شُيوخ   تاريخ   مُخْرِج   خِلال

Social/antisocial: This letter is social.

Shapes: How will you tell the خ apart from the previous two letters?

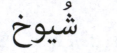

4	3	2	1
خ	ـخ	ـخـ	خـ

Activity 10   Practice writing *khaa'*   نشاط ١٠   تدريب على كتابة الخاء

Practice writing each form of خ as many times as you can across one line. Say the sound aloud as you write it.

خ

خـ

ـخـ

ـخ

As with the previous two letters, social letters that come before خ are sometimes written above the line. Practice writing the following words that show this, so that you can recognize this kind of combination.

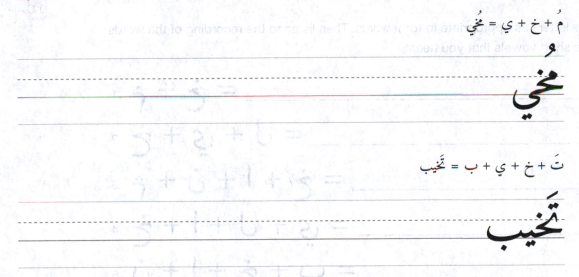

مُ + خ + ي = مُخي

مُخي

تَ + خ + ي + ب = تَخيب

تَخيب

What does this letter's appearance remind you of? How will you help yourself remember its sound? Draw a picture or write some notes here:

Activity 11 Reading practice: Where are the letters? (*jiim, Haa', and khaa'*)

نشاط ١١   تدريب على القراءة: أين الحروف؟ (الجيم والحاء والخاء)

Scan these lines from the poem "The Wretch Paused" by the classical Arab poet Abu Nuwas, and circle each instance you see of ج or ح or خ. All of these lines of poetry come from the same poem, but we have left out some lines in between them.

وعُجتُ أسألُ عن خمّارةِ البلدِ	عاجَ الشقيّ على دار يسائلها
ولا شفى وجدَ مَن يصبو إلى وتدِ	لا يُرقىءُ اللّهُ عينيْ مَن بكى حجراً
ليس الأعاريبُ عندَ اللّهِ من أحدِ	ومَن تميمٌ ومَن قيسٌ وإخوتُهم
لا تذخر اليوم شيئاً خوف فقر غدِ	اسمخْ وجُدْ بالذي تحْوي يداكَ لها

How many do you see of each? ج: _____   ح: _____   خ: _____

Activity 12 Letter connection practice: *khaa'*

نشاط ١٢   تدريب على ربط الحروف: الخاء

Connect the letters as appropriate to form words. Then listen to the recording of the words and add the short vowels that you hear.

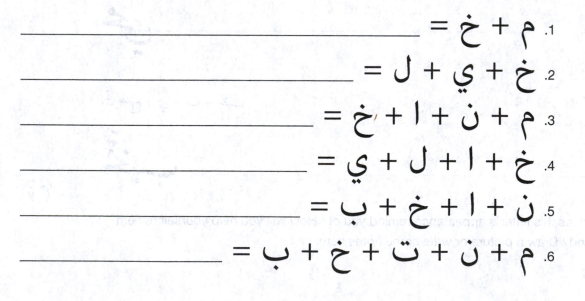

1. م + خ = _____

2. خ + ي + ل = _____

3. خ + ا + ن + م = _____

4. ي + ل + ا + خ = _____

5. ب + ا + خ + ن = _____

6. م + ن + ت + خ + ب = _____

Activity 13 Listening practice: *khaa', Haa', and haa'*

نشاط ١٣   تدريب على الاستماع: الخاء والحاء والهاء

You now know several letters that are easily confused with خ. In this exercise, you will practice hearing and recognizing the difference between letters that are formed deep in your throat.

You will hear a list of words. For each one, mark an X in the column that represents the sound you heard in that word. For example, if you hear the word أخي and you recognize the sound as a خ, put an X in the خ column. Some of the words may include sounds you have not studied yet—focus on which of these three letters you hear.

خ	هـ	ح	
			١.
			٢.
			٣.
			٤.
			٥.
			٦.
			٧.
			٨.
			٩.
			١٠.
			١١.
			١٢.

Activity 14 Listening and writing practice: jiim, Haa', and khaa'

نشاط ١٤   تدريب على الاستماع والكتابة: الجيم والحاء والخاء

Oops . . . someone forgot to include the dots when they wrote ج and خ! Both of these letters ended up looking like ح!

Listen to the *correct* version of the words below. If you see a letter ح that should actually be ج or خ, add a dot in the right place. If the letter ح is correct, do not add anything.

١. باحث

٢. ناحب

٣. محنون

٤. حاتم

٥. ثلوح

٦. حليب

٧. نحاحات

٨. حانت

٩. حوانب

١٠. حبايب

Activity 15 Practice reading *khaa'* نشاط ١٥ تدريب على قراءة الخاء

Practice reading these words containing خ and other letters out loud.

خَلَل   تَحْت   تَخْت

خالات   نُخَب   يَخون

Activity 16 Dictation practice: *khaa'*

نشاط ١٦   تدريب على الإملاء: الخاء

Listen to the dictation words and write them down as precisely as you can in Arabic letters.

_____ 1.

_____ 2.

_____ 3.

_____ 4.

_____ 5.

_____ 6.

_____ 7.

_____ 8.

_____ 9.

_____ 10.

The letter ع (*ᶜayn*) represents one of the most distinctive sounds in Arabic and is one of the most commonly occurring letters in the language. It represents a sound that does not exist in English, so it might take some time for you to be able to hear it and produce it correctly.

Letter name: عَين (*ᶜayn*)

Sound: This letter represents the sound made when you tighten the throat muscles in your neck, near your Adam's apple, at the same time as you make a sound like *ah*. Say the sound of the letter ع by yourself, checking with your teacher about how it sounds. ع is a consonant in Arabic that can come before or after any of the vowels. Listen to *ᶜayn* in the following words and repeat them aloud.

مَشْروع   مَع   بَعْدَ   عَن

Social/antisocial: This letter is social.

Shapes: Look at the different shapes for ᶜ*ayn* and identify the distinguishing features.

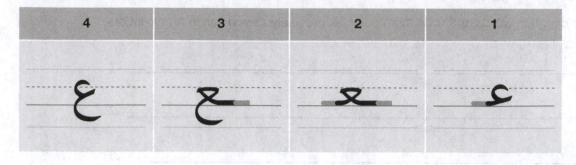

4	3	2	1
ع	ع	ع	ع

Activity 17 Practice writing ᶜ*ayn*   نشاط ١٧   تدريب على كتابة العين

Practice writing each form of the letter ع as many times as you can across one line. For the shapes of ᶜ*ayn* that come after social letters, make sure that the shape is not a rounded circle, but rather has a flattened top—this helps to distinguish it from other letters. Say the sound aloud as you write it.

ع

ع

ع

ع

    When coming after a social letter, the shape of عين is sometimes filled in and sometimes left open, depending on the style of handwriting or typeface. Look at the following font that uses the closed style and practice writing the letter this way. Then choose the way that you will use.

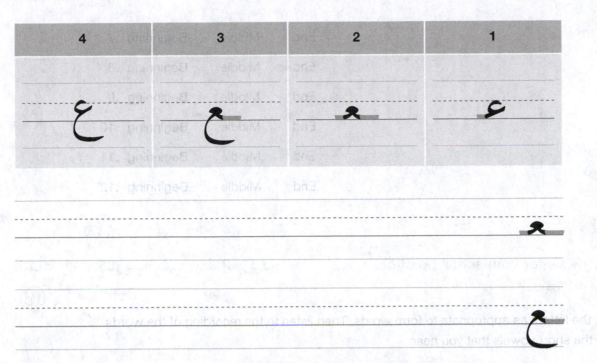

4	3	2	1
ع	ج	ـع	ع

What does this letter's appearance remind you of? How will you help yourself remember its shapes and sound? Draw a picture and write some notes here:

Activity 18 Listening practice:
       Where is the ʿayn?

نشاط ١٨   تدريب على الاستماع:
أين العين؟

Listen to twelve words that include the letter ع. Pause after each word and pronounce it yourself. Then, circle the appropriate word for whether you hear the letter ع at the **beginning**, **middle**, or **end** of the word.

End	Middle	Beginning .1
End	Middle	Beginning .2
End	Middle	Beginning .3
End	Middle	Beginning .4
End	Middle	Beginning .5
End	Middle	Beginning .6

End	Middle	Beginning .7
End	Middle	Beginning .8
End	Middle	Beginning .9
End	Middle	Beginning .10
End	Middle	Beginning .11
End	Middle	Beginning .12

Activity 19 Letter connection practice:
              ᶜayn

نشاط ١٩   تدريب على ربط الحروف:
          العين

Connect the letters as appropriate to form words. Then listen to the recording of the words and add the short vowels that you hear.

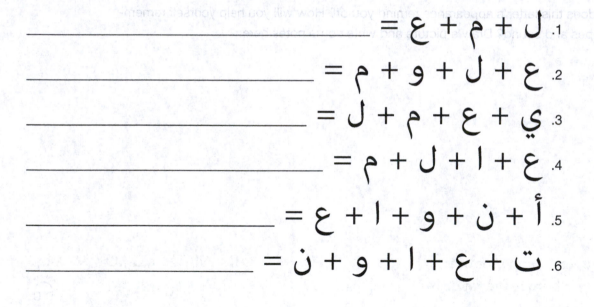

ل + م + ع = ‎.1 _____

ع + ل + و + م = ‎.2 _____

ل + م + ع + ي = ‎.3 _____

ع + ا + ل + م = ‎.4 _____

أ + ن + و + ا + ع = ‎.5 _____

ت + ع + ا + و + ن = ‎.6 _____

Activity 20 Listening practice: Vowels
              after *ᶜayn*

نشاط ٢٠   تدريب على الاستماع: الحركات
          بعد العين

In this exercise, you will practice hearing the letter عين in combination with different vowels. Because عين is a consonant, it can be followed by any of the long or short vowels in Arabic. First, listen to the following consonant-vowel combinations, read from right to left, and repeat them after the speaker:

عا   عو   عي   عَ   عُ   عِ

Now you will hear a series of words that include the letter عين. For each word, circle the combination of عين + vowel, from the six options listed below, that most closely matches what you hear. Remember to pay attention to whether the vowel following عين is a long or short vowel.

عِ	عُ	عَ	عي	عو	عا	.1
عِ	عُ	عَ	عي	عو	عا	.2
عِ	عُ	عَ	عي	عو	عا	.3
عِ	عُ	عَ	عي	عو	عا	.4
عِ	عُ	عَ	عي	عو	عا	.5
عِ	عُ	عَ	عي	عو	عا	.6
عِ	عُ	عَ	عي	عو	عا	.7
عِ	عُ	عَ	عي	عو	عا	.8

Activity 21 Reading and listening practice:
ᶜayn vs. hamza and alif

نشاط ٢١ تدريب على القراءة والاستماع:
العين مقابل الهمزة والألف

In this activity, you will practice reading and hearing how عين differs from both *hamza* and ألف, as these distinctions are often difficult for learners of Arabic.

Before listening

قبل الاستماع

First, read aloud each word in the chart below, making sure to note the differences in spelling and pronunciation between each pair. Check your pronunciations with your teacher.

أَن	عَن	.1
ما	مَع	.2

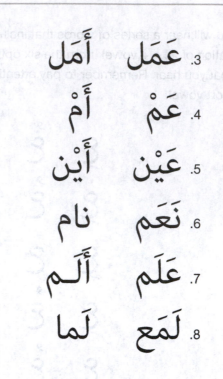

3. أَمَل عَمَل

4. أُمْ عَمْ

5. أَيْن عَيْن

6. نام نَعَم

7. أَلَـم عَلَم

8. لَما لَمَع

Listening الاستماع

Now, listen to the recording. From each numbered pair of words written in the chart above, you will hear only one word. Circle the word that you hear; then review your choices with your teacher.

After listening بعد الاستماع

After reviewing the correct answers, work with a classmate and challenge each other's reading and listening skills. One partner will choose a word at random and read it aloud; then the other partner will point to the word they heard in their own copy of the book. Check whether they got it right, then switch roles!

Activity 22 Practice reading ᵓayn نشاط ٢٢   تدريب على قراءة العين

Practice reading these words containing ع and other letters out loud.

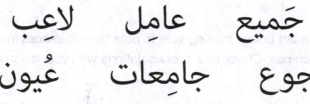

لاعِب عامِل جَميع

عُيون جامِعات جوع

Activity 23 Dictation practice: *ᶜayn*   نشاط ٢٣   تدريب على الإملاء: العين

Listen to the dictation words and write them down as precisely as you can in Arabic letters:

_____ .1

_____ .2

_____ .3

_____ .4

_____ .5

_____ .6

_____ .7

_____ .8

_____ .9

This letter represents another sound that is not found in English. It might take some time to develop the muscles in your throat used to make this sound, so be patient and keep practicing!

Letter Name: غَيْن (*ghayn*)

Sound: The letter غ represents a kind of "gargling" sound. French speakers may recognize it as similar to the way *r* is pronounced in that language. Move the very back of your tongue muscle toward the back of your throat and push air through this narrow passageway until the friction makes a trill. Listen to *ghayn* in the following words and repeat them aloud.

بَلاغ   صِيَغ   لُغَوِيّ   غَيْر

Social/antisocial: This letter is social.

Shapes: How are the shapes of *ghayn* different from the shapes of *ᶜayn*?

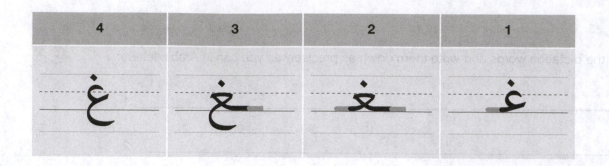

Activity 24 Practice writing *ghayn*   نشاط ٢٤   تدريب على كتابة الغين

Practice writing each form of غ as many times as you can across one line. For the shapes that come after social letters, make sure that the shape is not a rounded circle, but rather has a flattened top—this helps to distinguish it from other letters. Say the sound aloud as you write it.

Like *ʿayn*, the shape of *ghayn* is sometimes filled in and sometimes left open, depending on the style of handwriting or typeface. Look at the following font that uses the closed style and practice writing the letter this way. Then choose the way that you will use.

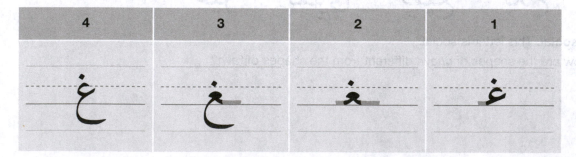

ـغـ

غ

What does this letter's appearance remind you of? How will you help yourself remember its shapes and sound? Draw a picture and write some notes here:

نشاط ٢٥   تدريب على القراءة: أين الحروف؟

Activity 25 Reading practice: Where are the letters?

Scan the following excerpt from the poem "On this Earth" by Palestinian poet Mahmoud Darwish. Draw a circle around each letter ع and a square around each letter غ.

على هذه الأرض ما يستحق الحياةْ: نهايةُ أيلولَ، سيّدةٌ تتركُ

الأربعين بكامل مشمشها، ساعة الشمس في السجن، غيمٌ يُقلّدُ

سِرباً من الكائنات، هتافاتُ شعب لمن يصعدون إلى حتفهم

باسمين، وخوفُ الطغاة من الأغنياتْ.

How many of each letter did you find? ع: _____. غ: _____.

Activity 26 Letter connection practice: *ghayn*   نشاط ٢٦   تدريب على ربط الحروف: الغين

Connect the letters as appropriate to form words. Then listen to the recording of the words and add the short vowels that you hear.

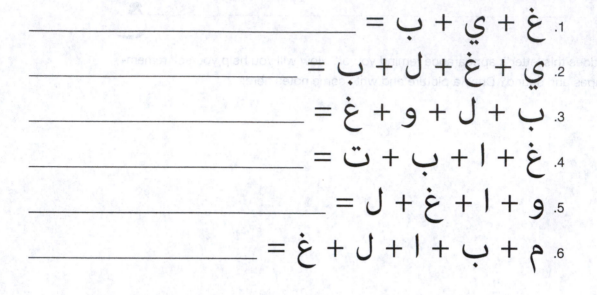

1. غ + ي + ب = _____

2. ب + ل + غ + ي = _____

3. غ + و + ل + ب = _____

4. ت + ب + ا + غ = _____

5. ل + غ + ا + و = _____

6. غ + ا + ل + ب + م = _____

Activity 27 Listening practice: *ᶜayn* vs. *ghayn*   نشاط ٢٧   تدريب على الاستماع: العين مقابل الغين

The ع and the غ represent very different sounds, but their similar shapes can be confusing. The following chart lists pairs of words that are similar sounding, but the first has ع and the second has غ. First, practice reading each of these words aloud. Then listen to the nine words in the recording and circle the word containing ع or غ depending on which word you hear from each pair.

1. غالي   عالي

2. غَيْب   عَيْب

3. غَيْن   عَيْن

4. أَنْغام   أَنْعام

5. نَغِل   نَعْل

6. بَعْل   بَغْل

7. وَعي   وَغي

8. عام   غام

9. نِعْمات   نَغَمات

Activity 28 Practice reading *ghayn*   نشاط ٢٨   تدريب على قراءة الغين

Practice reading these words containing غ and other letters out loud.

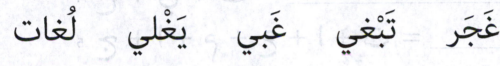

غَجَر   تَبْغي   غَبي   يَغْلي   لُغات

Activity 29 Dictation practice: *ghayn*   نشاط ٢٩   تدريب على الإملاء: الغين

Listen to the dictation words and write them down as precisely as you can in Arabic letters. 🎧

1. _____

2. _____

3. _____

4. _____

5. _____

6. _____

7. _____

8. _____

9. _____

REVIEW

المراجعة

Activity 30 Letter connection practice

نشاط ٣٠   تدريب على ربط الحروف

In this activity, you will review the letters from Part Three. Connect the letters as appropriate to form words. Then listen to the recording of the words and add the short vowels that you hear.

1. ن + ح + ن = _____

2. غ + ل + ب + ي = _____

3. ل + ا + ي + خ = _____

4. ث + ي + ح = _____

5. ج + ا + م + ع + ا + ت = _____

6. م + و + ي + غ = _____

7. م + ي + ل + ا + ع + ت = _____

8. خ + ا + ن + ا + ت = _____

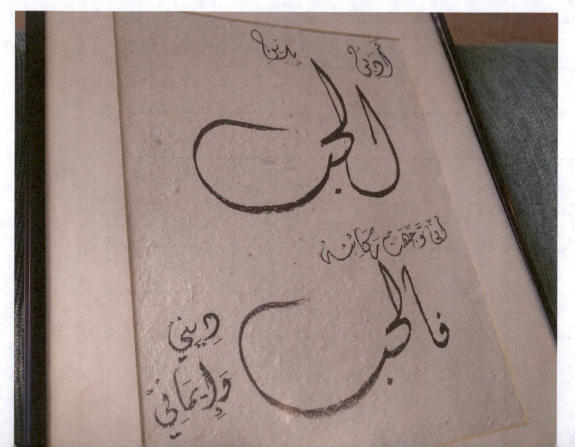

Activity 31 Practice reading handwriting

نشاط ٣١   تدريب على قراءة خط اليد

Practice reading these handwritten words out loud:

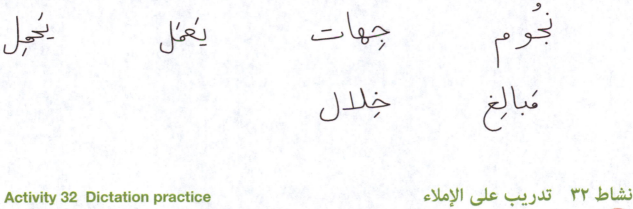

Activity 32 Dictation practice

نشاط ٣٢   تدريب على الإملاء

Listen to the dictation words and write them down as precisely as you can in Arabic letters.

_____ .1

_____ .2

_____ .3

_____ .4

_____ .5

_____ .6

_____ .7

_____ .8

PART FOUR

PART FOUR GOALS

الجزء الرابع

أهداف الجزء الرابع

By the end of this section, you should be able to do the following:

- Read, write, pronounce, and connect the consonants: س ش ر ز ف ق ك
- Review your skills with the letters that you have learned in previous lessons

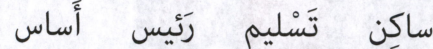

The letter س (*siin*) represents a sound that is common in both English and Arabic.

Letter name: سين (*siin*)

Sound: س represents an *s* sound. One way to make sure you are pronouncing this letter correctly is to make a wide smile while you say it. Listen to *siin* in the following words and repeat them aloud.

أَساس   رَئيس   تَسْليم   ساكِن

Social/antisocial: This letter is social.

Shapes: The letter س has four different shapes, all of which are recognizable by the three small "teeth" that poke above the line. At the end of a word, س has a distinctive tail.

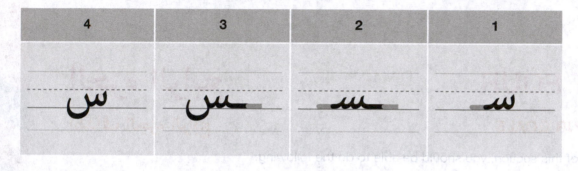

4	3	2	1
س	ـس	ـسـ	سـ

Activity 1   Practice writing *siin*   نشاط ١   تدريب على كتابة السين

Practice writing each form of س as many times as you can across one line, saying the sound aloud each time you write the letter. When writing the shape used at the end of a word, make sure that the tail of س curves back up, extending just above the line.

س also has a different appearance in some handwriting styles. Instead of exhibiting three "teeth," the letter is written as a horizontal line, longer than the letters around it. At the beginning of a word or after an anti-social letter, there is a small "hook" at the beginning of this letter.

4	3	2	1

Practice writing the handwriting forms of *siin*:

You can choose which kind of س you would like to write in your own handwriting. If you choose to write the "printed" forms, make sure that you are able to recognize the handwritten forms.

What does this letter's appearance remind you of? How will you help yourself remember its sound? Draw a picture and write some notes here:

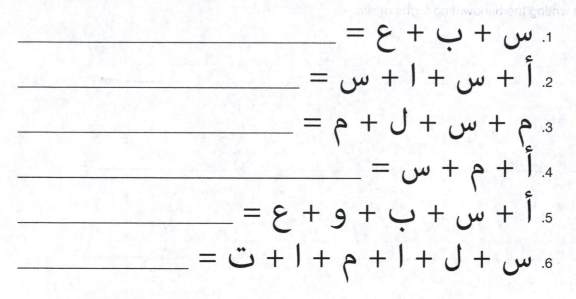

Activity 2   Letter connection practice:
siin

نشاط ٢   تدريب على ربط الحروف:
السين

Connect the letters as appropriate to form words. Then listen to the recording of the words and add the short vowels that you hear.

١. ع + ب + س = _____

٢. س + ا + س + أ = _____

٣. م + س + ل + م = _____

٤. س + م + أ = _____

٥. ع + و + ب + س + أ = _____

٦. ت + ا + م + ا + ل + س = _____

Activity 3   Practice reading *siin*

نشاط ٣   تدريب على قراءة السين

Practice reading the following words out loud. Remember to make your pronunciation of all short vowels very short and of all long vowels very long:

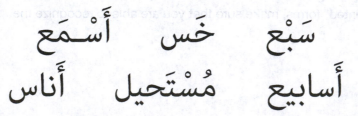

أَسْمَع   خَس   سَبْع

أَناس   مُسْتَحيل   أَسابيع

Activity 4   Dictation practice: *siin*

نشاط ٤   تدريب على الإملاء: السين

Listen to the dictation words and write them down as precisely as you can in Arabic letters:

_____ .1

_____ .2

_____ .3

_____ .4

_____ .5

_____ .6

_____ .7

_____ .8

_____ .9

**Activity 5   Dictation practice:
"My name is . . ."**

نشاط ٥   تدريب على الإملاء:
"اسمي..."

Before listening

قبل الاستماع

With the letter س you can now write the expression إِسمي, "my name." The letter ا at the beginning of this expression is pronounced as a short *i* sound, a *kasra*. For now, memorize the spelling and write a *kasra* under the *alif* to remember how it is pronounced. Write "my name" five times and pronounce it aloud as you write:

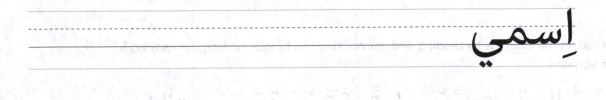

اِسمي

Listening

You will hear twelve sentences of people introducing themselves. Write what each person says, trying your best to spell any unfamiliar Arabic names. Your teacher can clarify the correct spelling of these names, as well as whether they are generally given to a particular gender.

_____ .1

_____ .2

_____ .3

_____ .4

_____ .5

_____ .6

_____ .7

_____ .8

_____ .9

_____ .10

_____ .11

_____ .12

Activity 6   Practice reading *siin* in context   تدريب على قراءة السين في جملة   نشاط ٦

Practice reading the letter س by reading and memorizing this tongue twister, then saying it as fast as you can.

خالْتي بَسْمَة بَسْبَسَتْ لي بَسْبوسة بِالسَّمْنة

It means, "My aunt Basma made me *basbuusa* with butter" (*basbuusa* is a kind of dessert).

The letter ش (shiin) represents a sound that is common to both Arabic and English.

Letter name: شين (shiin)

Sound: ش represents a *sh* sound. Listen to *shiin* in the following words and repeat them aloud.

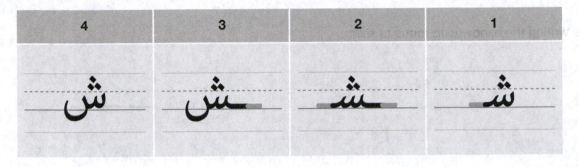

فَرْش   جَيْش   يُشير   شاشة

Social/antisocial: This letter is social.

Shapes: The shapes of the letter ش are very similar to those of س, except ش is written with three dots.

4	3	2	1
ش	ـش	ـشـ	شـ

Activity 7   Practice writing *shin*   نشاط ٧   تدريب على كتابة الشين

Practice writing each form of ش as many times as you can across one line, saying the sound aloud each time you write the letter. When writing the shape used at the end of a word, make sure that the tail of ش curves back up, extending just above the line.

The appearance of ش in some handwriting styles has elements in common with the letter س and the letter ث: The three "teeth" are replaced with a horizontal line (like س), while the three dots are replaced with a caret shape (like ث).

4	3	2	1

Practice writing the handwriting forms of *shiin*:

You can choose which kind of ش you would like to write in your own handwriting. If you choose to write the "printed" forms, make sure that you are able to recognize the handwritten forms.

What does this letter's appearance remind you of? How will you help yourself remember its sound? Draw a picture and write some notes here:

Connect the letters as appropriate to form words. Then listen to the recording of the words
and add the short vowels that you hear.

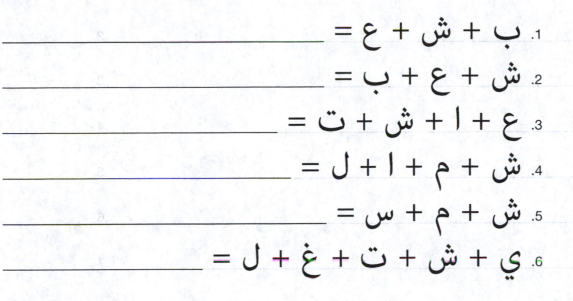

1. ع + ش + ب = _____

2. ب + ع + ش = _____

3. ت + ش + ا + ع = _____

4. ل + ا + م + ش = _____

5. س + م + ش = _____

6. ل + غ + ت + ش + ي = _____

نشاط ٩   تدريب على قراءة الشين   **Activity 9   Practice reading *shiin***

Practice reading the following words out loud. Remember to make your pronunciation of all
short vowels very short and of all long vowels very long:

شَيْخ   شَغَب   مَشْغُول

يَمْشِيان   شُيوعي   أَشْغال

For more practice with ش, memorize this tongue twister in Levantine Arabic and say it
as fast as you can:

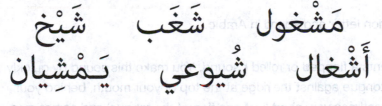

هاذا المِشْمِش مِش مِشْمِشْنا!

It means, "These apricots are not our apricots!"

Activity 10 Dictation practice: *shiin*   نشاط ١٠   تدريب على الإملاء: الشين

Listen to the dictation words and write them down as precisely as you can in Arabic letters:

_____ 1.

_____ 2.

_____ 3.

_____ 4.

_____ 5.

_____ 6.

_____ 7.

_____ 8.

_____ 9.

The letter ر (*raaʾ*) is a common letter and sound in Arabic.

Letter name: راء (*raaʾ*)

Sound: The letter ر represents a flapped or rolled *r* sound. You make this sound by quickly tapping the tip of your tongue against the ridge at the top of your mouth, behind your teeth. This sound is sometimes very short (just one flap of the tongue) and sometimes elongated (with your tongue repeatedly flapping, or trilling, at the top of your mouth). Practice both the short and elongated ر sounds.

There are certain consonants in Arabic that change the sound of vowels that appear near them in words. The letter ر is the first of these consonants you will learn. You can hear the effect of ر on surrounding vowels most clearly when it occurs near ا and *fatHa*: normally these are pronounced as "frontal" vowels (as in the English word *rat*), but near consonants like ر, their pronunciation becomes deeper (like the *a* sound in the English word *raw*). Another way to think about this is that the resonance or vibration of the vowel shifts from the front to the back your mouth, deep into your throat. Listen to *raa'* in the following words and repeat them aloud.

أَخْبار   أَمْر   عَرَبِيّ   رَجُل

Social/antisocial: This letter is antisocial.

Shapes: The ر has only two shapes. Both consist of a small, slightly curved line that starts above the line and hangs below.

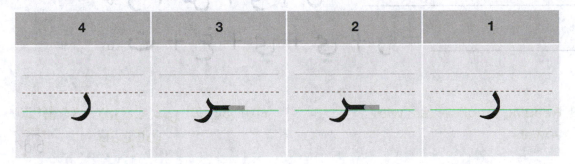

4	3	2	1
ر	ـر	ـر	ر

Activity 11   Practice writing *raa'*   نشاط ١١   تدريب على كتابة الراء

Practice writing each form of ر as many times as you can across one line, saying the sound aloud each time you write the letter. Make sure that the bottom end of ر stays below the line.

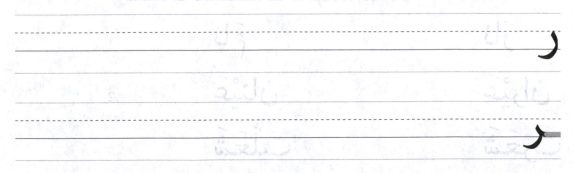

ر

ر

What does this letter's appearance remind you of? How will you help yourself remember its sound? Draw a picture and write some notes here:

Activity 12　Letter connection practice: *raa'*　　نشاط ١٢　تدريب على ربط الحروف: الراء

Connect the letters as appropriate to form words. Then listen to the recording of the words and add the short vowels that you hear.

١. أ + م + ر = _____

٢. ي + ب + ر + ع = _____

٣. ع + و + ر + ش + م = _____

٤. ر + ا + م + ع + أ = _____

٥. ل + و + س + ر = _____

٦. ر + ي + غ + ي + ت = _____

Activity 13　Reading practice: *raa'* with vowels　　نشاط ١٣　تدريب على القراءة: الراء والحركات

In this listening exercise, you will learn to recognize the way that the vowels ا and *fatHa* change in words that also contain the letter ر. With a partner, practice reading through the list of words, pair by pair. Remember that the words that contain ر have "deeper" vowels, while the words without ر have "lighter," frontal vowels. Then check your pronunciation by listening to the recording as you follow along and imitate the pronunciation that you hear.

Words with Deep Vowels	Words with Frontal Vowels	
نارَ	نامَ	١.
عَيْران	عَيْنان	٢.
شَعَرَت	شَعَلَت	٣.
غِيار	غِياب	٤.
رَبيع	تَبيع	٥.

Activity 14   Practice reading *raa'*   نشاط ١٤   تدريب على قراءة الراء

Practice reading these words containing ر out loud.

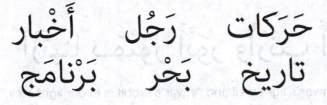

أَخْبار   رَجُل   حَرَكات

بَرْنامَج   بَحْر   تاريخ

Activity 15   Dictation practice: *raa'*   نشاط ١٥   تدريب على الإملاء: الراء

Listen to the dictation words and write them down as precisely as you can in Arabic letters:

1. _____

2. _____

3. _____

4. _____

5. _____

6. _____

7. _____

8. _____

9. _____

نشاط ١٦   تدريب على قراءة الراء في جملة   **Activity 16 Practice reading *raa'* in context**

Practice reading the letter ر by reading and memorizing this tongue twister, then saying it as fast as you can.

أَرْنَبنا بِـمَنْوَر أَنْوَر وَأَرْنَب أَنْوَر بِـمَنْوَرنا

It means, "Our rabbit is in Anwar's light-well and Anwar's rabbit is in our light-well."

The letter *zaay* (ز) represents a sound common to English and Arabic.

Letter name: زاي (*zaay*)

Sound: ز represents a *z* sound. Listen to *zaay* in the following words and repeat them aloud.

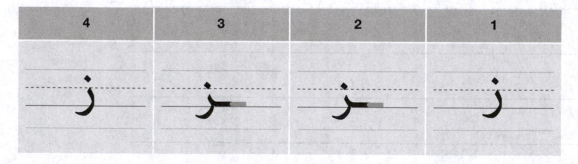

جِهاز   وِزارات   حِزْب   زالَ

Social/antisocial: This letter is antisocial.

Shapes: The letter ز has only two shapes. It has the same base shape as ر but with a dot above the letter.

4	3	2	1
ز	ـز	ـز	ز

نشاط ١٧   تدريب على كتابة الزاي   **Activity 17 Practice writing *zaay***

Practice writing each form of ز as many times as you can across one line, saying the sound aloud each time you write the letter. Make sure that the bottom end of the ز stays below the line.

What does this letter's appearance remind you of? How will you help yourself remember its sound? Draw a picture and write some notes here:

نشاط ١٨ تدريب على القراءة: أين الحروف؟ (الراء والزاي) — Activity 18 Reading practice: Where are the letters? (raa' and zay)

Scan these lines from the poem "Al-Mutanabbi to Sayf al-Dawla" by the classical Arab poet al-Mutanabbi, and circle each instance you see of ر and ز. These lines are all from the same poem, but they do not necessarily come consecutively in the original.

وتأتي على قدر الكرام المكارم	على قدر أهل العزم تأتي العزائم
فلما دنا منها سقتها الجماجم	سقتْها الغمامُ الغُرُّ قبل نزوله
إلى قول قومٍ أنت بالغيب عالم	تجاوزتَ مقدار الشجاعة والنُهى

How many do you see of each? ر: _____ ز: _____

نشاط ١٩ تدريب على ربط الحروف: الزاي — Activity 19 Letter connection practice: zaay

Connect the letters as appropriate to form words. Then listen to the recording of the words and add the short vowels that you hear.

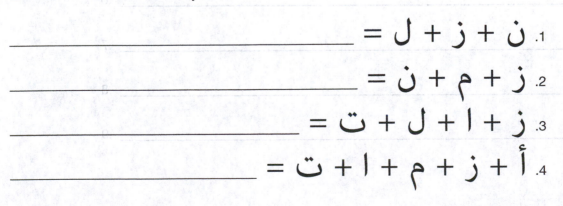

1. ن + ز + ل = _____

2. ز + م + ن = _____

3. ز + ا + ل + ت = _____

4. ت + ا + م + ز + أ = _____

5. ز + ر + ا + ع + ي = _____

6. م + ز + ا + ر + ع = _____

Activity 20 Practice reading *zaay*   نشاط ٢٠   تدريب على قراءة الزاي

Practice reading the following words out loud. Remember to make your pronunciation of all short vowels very short and of all long vowels very long:

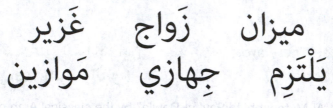

غَزير   زَواج   ميزان

مَوازين   جِهازي   يَلْتَزِم

Activity 21 Dictation practice: *zaay*   نشاط ٢١   تدريب على الإملاء: الزاي

Listen to the dictation words and write them down as precisely as you can in Arabic letters:

1. _____

2. _____

3. _____

4. _____

5. _____

6. _____

7. _____

8. _____

9. _____

Activity 22 Reading practice: "Family meal"

نشاط ٢٢   تدريب على القراءة: "الوجبة العائلية"

Read this mixed-up ad for a family meal combo from a restaurant and draw a line to connect each food item with the picture that it refers to.

　* Hint 1: Like the words "espresso" and "croissant" in English, the Arabic names for many food items from outside the Arab world are borrowed directly from other languages.

　* Hint 2: Because there is no letter *p* in Arabic, words with this sound often use the letter ب instead.

　Some words in this ad contain letters that you do not know yet. Using the other letters and the pictures, can you guess what those words say?

الوجبة العائلية!

بيتزا

برغر

صحن باستا

صحن سلطة

قنينتان بيبسي

كل هاد بـ15 دينار وبس!!

The letter *faa'* (ف) represents a sound that is also used in English.

Letter name: فاء (*faa'*)

Sound: The letter ف represents an *f* sound.

رُفوف   خَلْفَ   نَفْس   فَوْقَ

Social/antisocial: This letter is social.

Shapes: The letter ف is recognizable by its small loop with a dot above. Compare ف with the letter *miim* (م) and notice how the loop of this letter is different. The letter ف never drops below the line.

ف

🎧

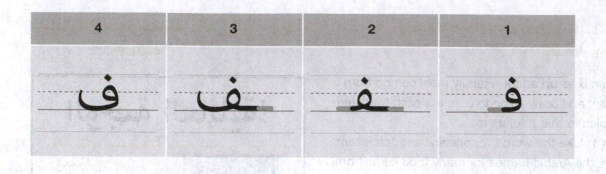

4	3	2	1
ف	ــف	ـف	ف

Activity 23 Practice writing *faa'*

نشاط ٢٣   تدريب على كتابة الفاء

Practice writing each form of ف as many times as you can across one line, saying the sound aloud each time you write the letter. Make sure that no part of the shape goes below the line.

	ف
	ف
	ـف
	ف

What does this letter's appearance remind you of? How will you help yourself remember its sound? Draw a picture and write some notes here:

Activity 24   Reading practice: Where are the letters? (*faa'* and *ghayn*)

نشاط ٢٤   تدريب على القراءة: أين الحروف؟ (الفاء والغين)

Scan these lines from the poem "Al-Mutanabbi to Sayf al-Dawla" by the classical Arab poet al-Mutanabbi, and circle each instance you see of ف and غ. These lines are all from the same poem, but they do not necessarily come consecutively in the original.

وتصغر في عين العظيم العظائم   تعظُمُ في عين الصغير صغارها

فلما دنا منها سقتها الجماجم   سقتْها الغمامُ الغُرُّ قبل نزوله

كأنك في جفن الردى وهو نائم   وقفتَ وما في الموت شكٌ لواقفٍ

How many do you see of each? ف: _____   غ: _____

Activity 25   Letter connection practice: *faa'*

نشاط ٢٥   تدريب على ربط الحروف: الفاء

Connect the letters as appropriate to form words. Then listen to the recording of the words and add the short vowels that you hear.

1. ف + ي = _____

2. س + ف + ن = _____

3. ف + ر + ع + ي = _____

4. ف + و + س = _____

5. ف + ي + ر + ش = _____

6. ع + ف + ت + ر + م = _____

Activity 26 Practice reading *faa'*   نشاط ٢٦   تدريب على قراءة الفاء

Practice reading the following words out loud. Remember to make your pronunciation of all short vowels very short and of all long vowels very long:

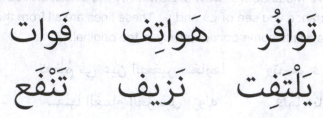

تَوافُر   هَواتِف   فَوات

يَلْتَفِت   نَزيف   تَنْفَع

Activity 27 Dictation practice: *faa'*   نشاط ٢٧   تدريب على الإملاء: الفاء

Listen to the dictation words and write them down as precisely as you can in Arabic letters:

1. _____

2. _____

3. _____

4. _____

5. _____

6. _____

7. _____

8. _____

9. _____

The letter *qaaf* (ق) represents a sound that is not found in English.

Letter name: قاف (*qaaf*)

Sound: In standard Arabic, ق represents a sound that is comparable to a *q* sound, but made deeper in your throat. Like the letter ر, the letter ق is one of the letters that change the sound of nearby vowels to a deeper tone. You will practice hearing and producing these different vowel sounds in the activities in that follow.

The letter *qaaf* is also a letter whose pronunciation varies significantly across different dialects. You will have the opportunity to learn more about this variation in relation to ق, as well as other letters, in a later section. Ask your teacher if you are curious to learn more now.

Listen to *qaaf* in the following words and repeat them aloud.

العِراق   صَديق   عَلاقات   قالَ

Social/antisocial: This letter is social.

Shapes: The shapes of ق are similar to those of ف, but they are notably different at the end of a word: the tail of ق drops below the line.

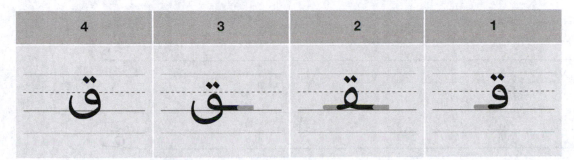

4	3	2	1
ق	ـق	ـقـ	قـ

Activity 28 Practice writing *qaaf*   نشاط ٢٨   تدريب على كتابة القاف

Practice writing each form of ق as many times as you can across one line, saying the sound aloud each time you write the letter.

قـ

ـقـ

ـق

ق

The handwriting shapes for the letter ق follow a similar principle to those of the letter ت: the two dots above the letter are commonly replaced by a straight line.

4	3	2	1
ـق	ـق	ـة	ق

Practice the handwriting forms for ق:

ق

ـة

ـق

ـق

You can choose which kind of ق you would like to write in your own handwriting. If you choose to write the "printed" forms, make sure that you are able to recognize the handwritten forms.

What does this letter's appearance remind you of? How will you help yourself remember its sound? Draw a picture and write some notes here:

Activity 29 Letter connection practice:
　　　　　　　qaaf

نشاط ٢٩　تدريب على ربط الحروف:
　　　　　　القاف

Connect the letters as appropriate to form words. Then listen to the recording of the words and add the short vowels that you hear.

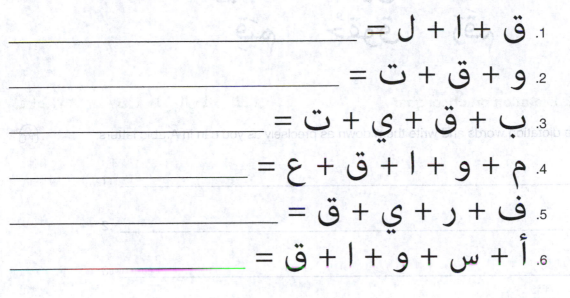

١. ق + ا + ل = ـ_____

٢. ت + ق + و = _____

٣. ت + ي + ق + ب = _____

٤. ع + ا + ق + و + م = _____

٥. ق + ي + ر + ف = _____

٦. ق + ا + و + س + أ = _____

Activity 30 Reading practice: qaaf with
　　　　　　　vowels

نشاط ٣٠　تدريب على القراءة: القاف
　　　　　　　والحركات

In this exercise, you will learn to recognize how the vowels ‌ا and *fatHa* change in words that contain the letter ق. With a partner, practice reading through the list of words, pair by pair. Remember that the words that contain ق have "deeper" vowels, while the words without ق have "lighter," frontal vowels. Then check your pronunciation by listening to the recording as you follow along and copy the pronunciation that you hear.

١. قالَت　نالَت

٢. سابِق　سابِع

٣. نَقْل　نَمْل

٤. قَتيل　فَتيل

٥. قالِب　غالِب

Activity 31   Practice reading *qaaf*   نشاط ٣١   تدريب على قراءة القاف

Practice reading these words containing ق out loud.

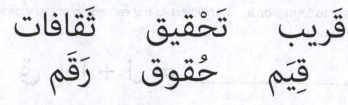

ثَقافات   تَحْقيق   قَريب

رَقَم   حُقوق   قِيَم

Activity 32   Dictation practice: *qaaf*   نشاط ٣٢   تدريب على الإملاء: القاف

Listen to the dictation words and write them down as precisely as you can in Arabic letters:

_____ 1.

_____ 2.

_____ 3.

_____ 4.

_____ 5.

_____ 6.

_____ 7.

_____ 8.

_____ 9.

The letter *kaaf* (ك) represents a sound that is common in English as well as Arabic.

Letter name: كاف (*kaaf*)

Sound: ك represents a hard *k* sound. Unlike ق, this sound does not come from deep in your throat, and it does not change the sound of the vowels around it—the ا and the *fatHa* stay "bright."

مُديرُكِ   كِتابُكَ   حُكومات   كانَت

Social/antisocial: This letter is social.

Shapes: The shapes of the letter *kaaf* vary significantly. For two of its forms, *kaaf* has two
  pieces: a bottom piece slanting to the left and a top piece slanting to the right. The bottom piece is written first and connects with the other letters in the word, while the top
  piece is written after finishing all the base shapes in the word—the same way that dots
  for other letters are written after the whole word shape is written.

The final shapes of ك have a small squiggle written in the middle of a shape that is
somewhat similar to *laam*. Unlike the shapes of the letter ل, however, these final shapes do
not drop below the line.

4	3	2	1
ك	ـك	ـكـ	كـ

Activity 33 Practice writing *kaaf*   نشاط ٣٣   تدريب على كتابة الكاف

Practice writing each form of ك as many times as you can across one line, saying the
sound aloud each time you write the letter. For the first two shapes, make sure to add each
shape's top piece *after* writing its bottom piece. For the final shapes, make sure that they
do not drop below the line.

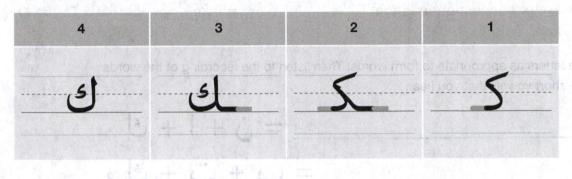

What does this letter's appearance remind you of? How will you help yourself remember its sound? Draw a picture and write some notes here:

Activity 34 Letter connection practice: *kaaf*

نشاط ٣٤ تدريب على ربط الحروف: الكاف

Connect the letters as appropriate to form words. Then listen to the recording of the words and add the short vowels that you hear.

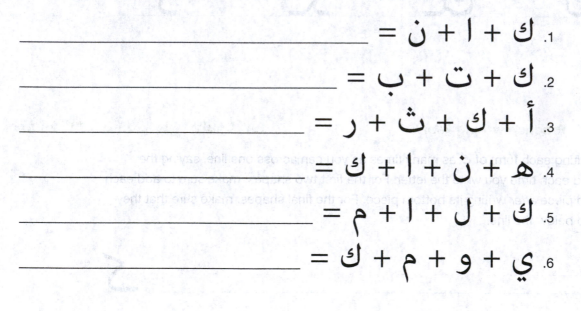

1. ك + ا + ن = _____

2. ك + ت + ب = _____

3. أ + ك + ث + ر = _____

4. ك + ا + ن + ه = _____

5. م + ا + ل + ك = _____

6. ي + و + م + ك = _____

Activity 35 Practice reading and listening: *qaaf* vs. *kaaf*

نشاط ٣٥ تدريب على القراءة والاستماع: القاف مقابل الكاف

In this drill, you will practice reading and hearing the difference between ق and ك.

Before listening

قبل الاستماع

First, read aloud each word in the chart below, making sure to note the differences in spelling and pronunciation between each pair. Remember that not only is the consonant itself a different sound, it also changes some of the vowels around it. Check your pronunciations with your teacher.

1. قَلْب   كَلْب

2. قانون   كانون

3. فَريق   فَريك

4. يُبْقي   يُبْكي

5. تَقْرير   تَكْرير

6. شَوْق   شَوْك

7. فَقْر   فَكْر

8. شِراق   شِراك

9. قَتَلَت   كَتَلَت

الاستماع

Listening

Now, listen to the recording of the nine words and circle the word that you hear from each pair.

بعد الاستماع

After listening

After reviewing the correct answers, work with a classmate and challenge each other's reading and listening skills. Let one partner choose a word at random and read it aloud; then let the other partner point to the word they heard in their own copy of the book. Check whether they got it right, then switch roles!

نشاط ٣٦   تدريب على قراءة الكاف   Activity 36   Practice reading *kaaf*

Practice reading these words containing ك out loud.

هُناك   أَحْكي   زَوْجُكِ

حُكومات   كُرات   مَحاكِم

Listen to the dictation words and write them down as precisely as you can in Arabic letters:

_____ .1

_____ .2

_____ .3

_____ .4

_____ .5

_____ .6

_____ .7

_____ .8

_____ .9

Activity 38 Practice reading *kaaf*, *raa'*,   نشاط ٣٨ تدريب على قراءة الكاف والراء
and *Haa'* in context   والحاء في الجملة

Read this tongue twister out loud several times over. Try to read a little bit faster each time, while still pronouncing the letter ح correctly! There is one letter in this tongue twister that you have not yet learned: the letter ط. Pronounce this letter like a ت that comes from much further back in your mouth. You will study this letter in detail later in this book.

Don't give in to the temptation to write the tongue twister out in English letters! You'll never get good at reading Arabic that way.

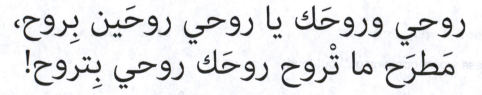

روحي وروحَك يا روحي روحَين بِروح،
مَطرَح ما تْروح روحَك روحي بِتروح!

It means, "My soul and your soul are one soul. Wherever your soul goes, my soul also goes!"

REVIEW AND EXPANSION

المراجعة والتوسيع

In this section you will review the letters that you have learned and test your new skills.

Activity 39 Letter connection practice

نشاط ٣٩   تدريب على ربط الحروف

Connect the letters as appropriate to form words. Then listen to the recording of the words and add the short vowels that you hear.

1. ل + ا + ع + ب = _____

2. غ + ا + ل + ب = _____

3. ي + ش + م + ت = _____

4. ر + و + ه + ش = _____

5. ر + س + أ = _____

6. ي + ل + ا + ع + ت = _____

7. ت + ا + و + ن + س = _____

8. ش + ي + ا + ع + ت = _____

9. ز + ك + ا + ر + م = _____

10. ت + ع + ز + ي + ز + ت = _____

Activity 40 Practice reading handwriting

نشاط ٤٠   تدريب على قراءة خط اليد

Practice reading these handwritten words out loud.

كَلِمات   أمس   شَعب   عَشَرات

قَوافِل   قِرش   مَراكِز   تِلكَ

تَعزيز   شَكل

Activity 41 Dictation practice
نشاط ٤١   تدريب على الإملاء 🎧

Listen to the dictation words and write them down as precisely as you can in Arabic letters.

_____ 1.

_____ 2.

_____ 3.

_____ 4.

_____ 5.

_____ 6.

_____ 7.

_____ 8.

_____ 9.

_____ 10.

Activity 42 Practice writing names
نشاط ٤٢   تدريب على كتابة الأسماء

Who in your class has any of the following sounds in their names? Sound out and write as many classmates' names as possible on a separate sheet of paper. Are there any class-mates' names that you do not know the letters for yet?

ش   ج   س   ر   ك

Activity 43 Reading practice: The biggest American cities
نشاط ٤٣   تدريب على القراءة: أكبر المدن الأمريكية

Uh oh! Someone erased some of the names from the list of the largest US cities on Wikipe-dia.* Luckily, you're here to fix them.

*https://en.wikipedia.org/wiki/List_of_United_States_cities_by_population

1. Connect the letters of the missing cities and sound them out to figure out what cities are missing. The missing cities:

1. س + ا + ن + خ + و + س + ي + ه =

_____

2. س + ف + م + ي + م =

_____

3. ف + و + ر + ت   ت + و + ر + ث =

_____

4. ف + ي + ن + ك + س =

_____

5. ن + ي + و + ي + و + ر + ك =

_____

6. ج + ا + ك + س + و + ن + ف + ي + ل =

_____

7. ش + ي + ك + ا + غ + و =

_____

8. س + ي + ا + ت + ل =

_____

2. Fill in the blank spaces in the chart below with the names of the missing cities from above. Use your knowledge of these cities' sizes and of the states where they are located to place them in the correct blanks.

3. Challenge: Deduce the name of every city and state on the chart, even if you do not know all the letters in these words yet!

عدد السكان (تقديرات 2015)	الولاية	المدينة	الترتيب
8,550,405	نيويورك	_____	1
3,971,883	كاليفورنيا	لوس أنجلس	2
2,720,546	إلينوي	_____	3
2,296,224	تكساس	هيوستن	4
1,567,442	بنسلفانيا	فيلادلفيا	5
1,563,025	أريزونا	_____	6
1,469,845	تكساس	سان أنطونيو	7
1,394,928	كاليفورنيا	سان دييغو	8
1,300,092	تكساس	دالاس	9
1,026,908	كاليفورنيا	_____	10
931,830	تكساس	أوستن	11
868,031	فلوريدا	_____	12
864,816	كاليفورنيا	سان فرانسيسكو	13
853,173	إنديانا	إندianابوليس	14
850,106	أوهايو	كولومبوس	15
833,319	تكساس	_____	16

عدد السكان (تقديرات 2015)	الولاية	المدينة	الترتيب
827,097	نورث كارولينا	شارلوت	17
684,451	واشنطن	────────	18
682,545	كولورادو	دنفر	19
681,124	تكساس	إل باسو	20
677,116	ميشيغان	ديترويت	21
672,228	واشنطن العاصمة	واشنطن	22
667,137	ماساتشوسيتس	بوسطن	23
655,770	تينيسي	────────	24
654,610	تينيسي	ناشفيل	25

PART FIVE

الجزء الخامس

أهداف الجزء الخامس

PART FIVE GOALS

By the end of this section, you should be able to do the following:

- Read, write, pronounce, and connect: ة

- Read, write, pronounce, and connect the letters: د ذ أ إ

- Write and pronounce the symbol *shadda*: ّ

ة

The letter *taa' marbuuTa* (ة) is a kind of *taa'* that occurs only at the end of nouns and adjectives. It is not considered a separate letter among the twenty-eight principal letters of the Arabic alphabet, but it plays a very important role in Arabic script and grammar. When it occurs at the end of a word, it usually indicates that the noun or adjective is grammatically feminine.

Letter name: تاء مربوطة (*taa' marbuuTa*)

Sound: ة is sometimes pronounced as a هـ and sometimes as a ت. It always comes after a *fatHa* (a) sound, so it sounds either like a short *ah* or a short *at*. Listen to *taa' marbuuTa* as *ah* in the following words and repeat them aloud.

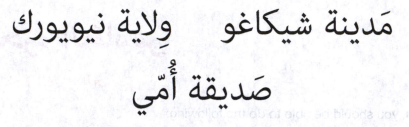

مُمْتازة   ثانِية   ساعة   سَنة

Now, listen to *taa' marbuuTa* as *at* in the following words and repeat them aloud.

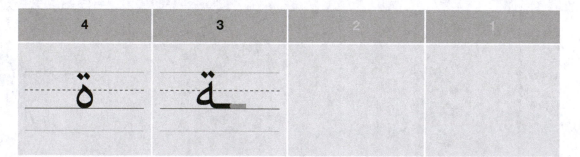

مَدينة شيكاغو   وِلاية نيويورك

صَديقة أُمّي

You will learn more about the rules for these different pronunciations elsewhere. For now, when you **hear** a word that ends in an *ah* or a sound, you can assume that it ends in ة (this is true for many words). When you **read** a new word in a vocabulary list that ends in ة, the basic pronunciation will be *ah*.

Social/antisocial: Not applicable.

Shapes: ة only appears at the end of words, which means that it only has two shapes: one for when it comes after a social letter and the other for when it comes after an antisocial letter. How are the shapes for ة similar to and different from other letters?

4	3	2	1
ة	ـة		

Activity 1 Practice writing *taa' marbuuTa* نشاط ١ تدريب على كتابة التاء المربوطة

Practice writing each form of ة as many times as you can across one line, saying the sound aloud each time you write it.

ـة

ة

Like the letter *taa'*, *taa' marbuuTa* can be written in handwriting with a line in place of the two dots.

4	3	2	1
ة	ـة		

Practice writing the handwriting forms of ة.

ـة

ة

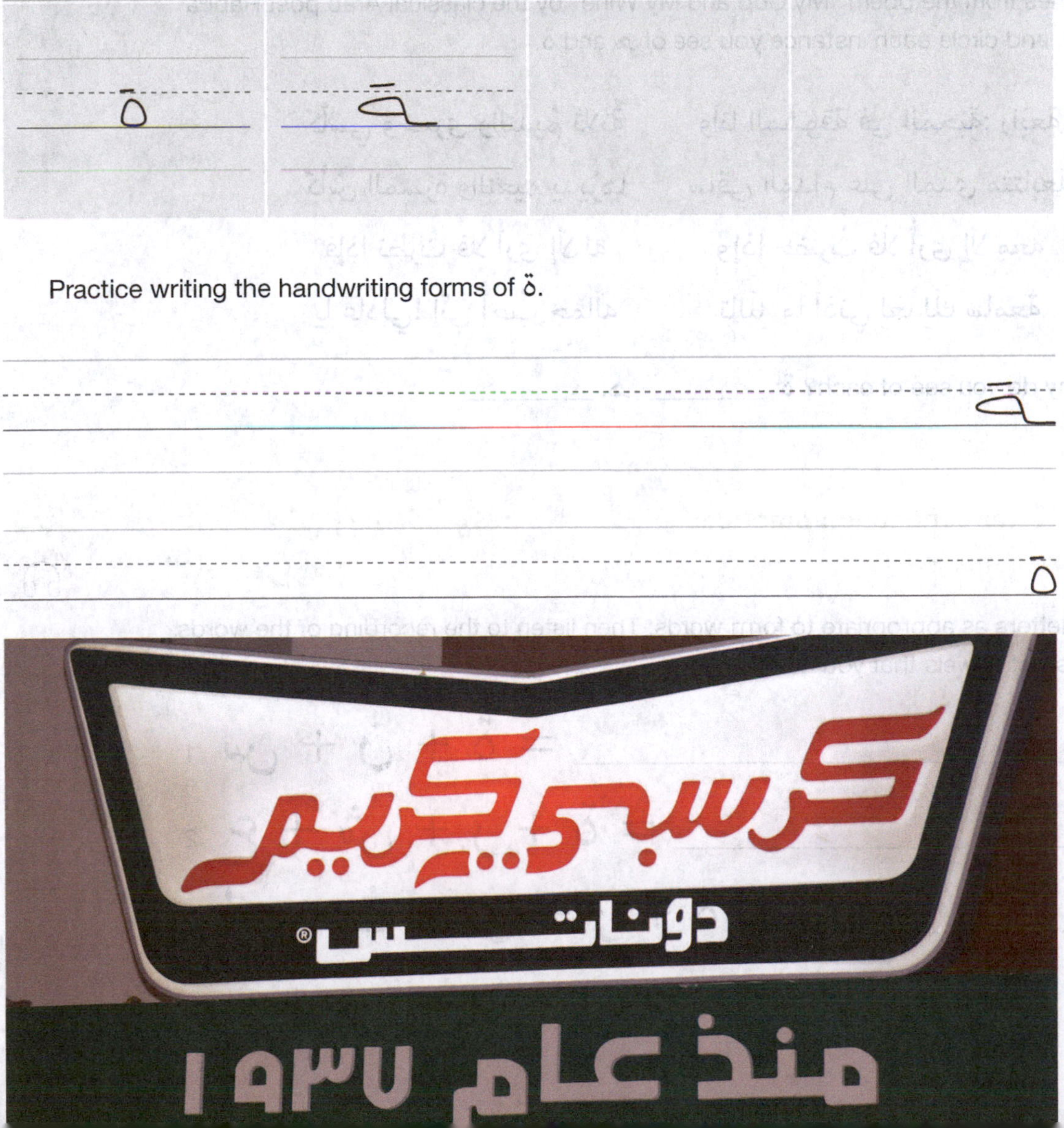

You can choose which kind of ة you would like to write in your own handwriting, but make sure that you are able to recognize both forms.

What does this letter's appearance remind you of? How will you help yourself remember its sound? Draw a picture and write some notes here:

Activity 2 Reading practice: Where are the letters? (*haa'* and *taa' marbuuta*)	نشاط ٢ تدريب على القراءة: أين الحروف؟ (الهاء والتاء المربوطة)

Scan these lines from the poem "My Cup and My Wine" by the classical Arab poet Rabi⸱a al-⸱Adawiyya, and circle each instance you see of ﻫ and ة.

كأسي وخمري والنديمُ ثلاثةٌ   وأنا المشوقة في المحبّةِ: رابعة

كأسُ المسرّةِ والنعيم يديرُها   ساقي المدامِ على المدى متتابعة

فإذا نظرتُ فلا أُرى إلّا له   وإذا حضرتُ فلا أرى إلّا معه

يا عاذلي! إنّي أُحبُّ جمالَه   تاللّهِ ما أُذني لِعَذْلِكَ سامعة

How many do you see of each? ة: _____ ﻫ: _____

Activity 3 Letter connection practice: *taa' marbuuTa*	نشاط ٣ تدريب على ربط الحروف: التاء المربوطة

Connect the letters as appropriate to form words. Then listen to the recording of the words and add the short vowels that you hear.

١. س + ن + ة = _____

٢. ع + ش + ر + ة = _____

٣. ك + ث + ي + ر + ة = _____

٤. ث + ل + ا + ث + ة = ــــــــــــــــ

٥. ع + ز + ي + ز + ة = ــــــــــــــــ

٦. ث + ا + ن + ي + ة = ــــــــــــــــ

نشاط ٤ تدريب على قراءة التاء المربوطة   **Activity 4 Practice reading *taa' marbuuTa***

Practice reading the following words out loud. Remember to make your pronunciation of all short vowels very short and of all long vowels very long:

أَميرة   خَمسة   لازِمة

زُجاجة   ثَقافة   وَرَقة

نشاط ٥ تدريب على الإملاء: التاء المربوطة   **Activity 5 Dictation practice: *taa' marbuuTa***

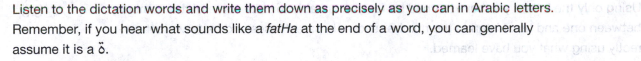

Listen to the dictation words and write them down as precisely as you can in Arabic letters. Remember, if you hear what sounds like a *fatHa* at the end of a word, you can generally assume it is a ة.

ــ ١.

ــ ٢.

ــ ٣.

ــ ٤.

ــ ٥.

ــ ٦.

ــ ٧.

_____ .8

_____ .9

Activity 6   Practice reading *taa' marbuuTa* in context

نشاط ٦   تدريب على قراءة التاء المربوطة في الجملة

For more practice with ة, try reading and memorizing this tongue twister, and then say it as fast as you can. (You will need to ask your teacher how to pronounce the word with the letter ط.) All instances of *taa' marbuuTa* in this tongue twister are pronounced as ت.

مَرَقة رَقَبة بَقَرتنا أَطْيَب مِن مَرَقة رَقَبة بَقَرة عَمَّتنا.

It means, "The broth made from our cow's neck is tastier than the broth made from our uncle's cow's neck."

Activity 7   Practice writing numbers

نشاط ٧   تدريب على كتابة الأعداد

Using only the letters you have learned so far, you are able to write some of the numbers between one and ten. Listen to the number shown in parentheses and try to write it correctly using what you have learned.

_____

_____ (3)

_____

_____ (4)

_____

_____ (6)

_____

_____ (8)

_____ (9)

_____ (10)

Letter name: دال (*daal*)

Sound: This letter is similar to an English *d* sound, pronounced with your tongue touching the ridge behind your upper teeth, as in *dog*. Listen to *daal* in the following words and repeat them aloud:

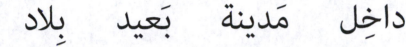

بِلاد   بَعيد   مَدينة   داخِل

Social/antisocial: This letter is antisocial.

Shapes: As an anti-social letter, *daal* has only two shapes. Compare the shapes of *daal* to those of the letter *raa'*: how are these two letters similar and different?

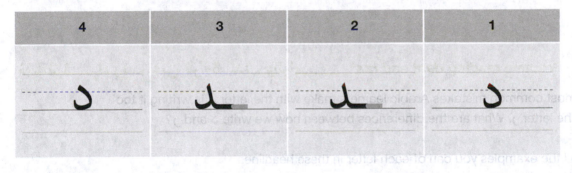

4	3	2	1
د	ـد	ـد	د

Activity 8   Practice writing *daal*   نشاط ٨   تدريب على كتابة الدال

Practice writing each form of د as many times as you can across one line, saying the sound as you write. Remember that this shape never drops below the line.

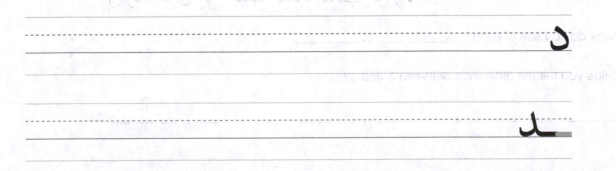

د

ـد

Now practice writing the different forms of ر again, just to make sure you can consistently distinguish between the two letters.

ر

ــر

What does the appearance of the letter د remind you of? How will you help yourself remember its sound? Draw a picture or write some notes here:

Activity 9   Practice reading *daal* and *raa'*   نشاط ٩   تدريب على قراءة الدال والراء

One of the most common mistakes Arabic learners make with the letter د is writing it too similarly to the letter ر. What are the differences between how we write د and ر؟

1. Circle all the examples you can of each letter in these headlines.
2. Jot down the key differences between the two letters.

تقرير جديد: يمدد ديفيد برون رحلته حول أوروبا

فيديو جديد من إسكندر عبد الرزاق في الدار البيضاء

زيارة أخرى إلى مدينة بغداد لنائب الوزراء

How many do you see of each? ر: _____   د: _____

What helps you tell the difference between د and ر؟

_____

Activity 10 Letter connection practice:
daal

نشاط ١٠ تدريب على ربط الحروف:
الدال

Connect the letters as appropriate to form words. Then listen to the recording of the words and add the short vowels that you hear.

١. د + ف + ا + ع = _____

٢. ش + د + ي + د = _____

٣. د + و + ل + ة = _____

٤. ز + ي + ا + د + ة = _____

٥. ب + ع + د = _____

Activity 11 Practice reading *daal*

نشاط ١١ تدريب على قراءة الدال

Practice reading these words containing د out loud:

يَد   بارِد   دَعم   رَد

مَديح   داخل   عَدَد

Activity 12 Practice writing *daal* in names

نشاط ١٢ تدريب على كتابة الدال في الأسماء

Who in your class has a د sound in their name? If no one does, how about a famous person with a د sound in their name? Spell out their names in Arabic:

_____

_____

_____

_____

Activity 13 Dictation practice: *daal*   نشاط ١٣   تدريب على الإملاء: الدال

Listen to the dictation words and write them down as exactly as you can in Arabic letters:

_____ .1

_____ .2

_____ .3

_____ .4

_____ .5

_____ .6

_____ .7

_____ .8

_____ .9

_____ .10

Letter name: ذال (*dhaal*)

Sound: The letter ذ sounds like the *th* sound in *then*, *this*, and *bother*.* Note that the *th* sound in *this* is different than the *th* sound in *thin*. In English, the letter combination *th* makes more than one sound: compare the words "thigh" (ث) and "thy" (ذ). In this book, we use the combination "dh" to represent the letter ذ when writing Arabic words in English letters. Can you think of other English words that have a ذ sound in them? Listen to *dhaal* in the following words and repeat them aloud.

أُسْتاذ   مُنْذُ   لِماذا   ذِكْرَيات

Social/antisocial: This letter is antisocial.

---

*If you learned the expression عن إذنك in a dialect, you will notice that the letter ذ sometimes sounds like ز in spoken Arabic. In Part Seven, you will learn more about the sound changes that take place with the letters in different dialects.

Shapes: How are the shapes of *dhaal* different from the shapes of *daal*?

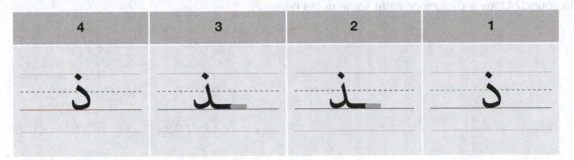

4	3	2	1
ذ	ـذ	ـذ	ذ

Activity 14 Practice writing *dhaal*   نشاط ١٤   تدريب على كتابة الذال

Practice writing each form of ذ as many times as you can across one line, saying the sound aloud as you write. Remember that this shape never drops below the line.

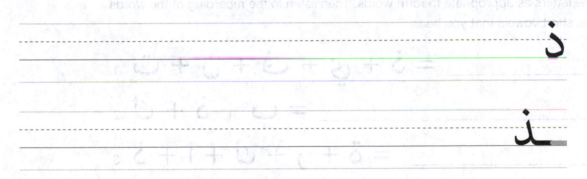

ذ

ـذ

Now practice writing the different forms of ز again, just to make sure you can consistently distinguish between the two letters:

ز

ـز

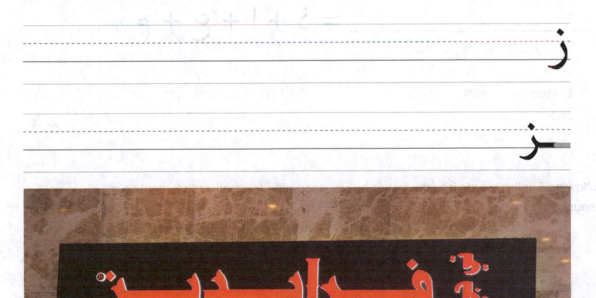

What does the appearance of the letter ذ remind you of? How will you help yourself remember its sound? Draw a picture or write some notes here:

Activity 15 Letter connection practice: *dhaal*

نشاط ١٥   تدريب على ربط الحروف: الذال

Connect the letters as appropriate to form words. Then listen to the recording of the words and add the short vowels that you hear.

١. ت + ن + ف + ي + ذ = _____

٢. ك + ذ + ب = _____

٣. ذ + ا + ك + ر + ة = _____

٤. ق + ذ + ي + ف + ة = _____

٥. م + ع + ا + ذ = _____

Activity 16 Listening practice: *dhaal* v. *thaa'*

نشاط ١٦   تدريب على الاستماع: الذال مقابل الثاء

Before listening

قبل الاستماع

Sort the following English words into the boxes below, according to whether they contain a ث or a ذ sound.

brother   thud   sloth   ethical   feather   this
myth   then   thin   though   thorough

ث	ذ

Listening

الاستماع

Practice hearing and recognizing the difference between the letters ذ and ث in Arabic words. You will hear a list of words. For each one, make a check mark in the column that represents the sound you hear in that word. For example, if you hear the word ذلك and you recognize the sound as a ذ, put a check in the ذ column.

ث	ذ	
		.1
		.2
		.3
		.4
		.5
		.6
		.7
		8.
		.9
		.10

Activity 17 Practice reading *dhaal* نشاط ١٧ تدريب على قراءة الذال

Practice reading these words containing د, ذ, ث, ر, and ز out loud.

دَبابة   ذاب   جُثَث

رَد   زَيت   شَديد   زِر

يَذوب   وِراثة   زيارة

Activity 18 Dictation practice: *dhaal*   نشاط ١٨   تدريب على الإملاء: الذال

Listen to the dictation words and write them down as precisely as you can in Arabic letters. Be careful—not every word contains the letter ذ.

_____ .1

_____ .2

_____ .3

_____ .4

_____ .5

_____ .6

_____ .7

_____ .8

_____ .9

_____ .10

In Part One, you learned that the short vowel sounds in Arabic are represented by three different symbols written above or below letters: *a* is represented by *fatHa* (◌َ), *i* by *kasra* (◌ِ), and *u* by *Damma* (◌ُ). When the short vowel sound *a* occurs at the beginning of a word, you learned that its corresponding symbol, *fatHa* (◌َ), must be written above both an *alif* (ا) and a *hamza* symbol (ء): أ.

أُعْ
أ

إِ

When we want to write the other short vowel symbols at the beginning of a word, the same principle applies: we must write them with *alif* and *hamza*. It may be useful to think of these combinations as the way to write the three short vowels at the beginning of words. They represent the same sounds that short vowel symbols represent in other places in words. More technically, these combinations are all considered to be varieties of *hamza*. Listen to *hamza* at the beginning of the following words and repeat them aloud:

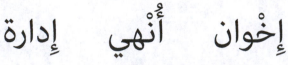

إدارة   أُنْهي   إخْوان   أُحِبّ

Remember that the *alif* shape here does not make an *aa* sound but rather serves as a placeholder or "platform" for the short vowels. Notice that in the combination representing a short *i* sound, with *kasra*, the *hamza* shape is written below the *alif*: إٕ.

Because people usually do not write the short vowels in texts, it can sometimes be difficult to know exactly how to pronounce an *alif* at the beginning of a word. We recommend that you always write all the symbols with words when you are learning them, as this will help you to remember the pronunciation of words that you have learned.

Activity 19 Practice writing *Damma* and   نشاط ١٩   تدريب على كتابة الضمة
           kasra* on *alif-hamza*   والكسرة على الهمزة والألف

Practice writing أٌ and إٕ across the lines below, saying the sound of each aloud as you write.

أٌ

إٕ

What do these letter and symbol combinations remind you of? How will you help yourself remember their sounds? Draw a picture or write some notes here:

Activity 20 Listening practice: *hamza* **at**
the beginning of words

Someone forgot to write the ء and short vowels on the ا at the beginning of each of these
words. Listen to the words and add the ء and all the short vowels you hear, both on the ء
or on other letters in each word.

١. اذا

٢. احب

٣. اخ

٤. اسبوع

٥. انهي

٦. اساتذة

٧. اسلام

٨. اخوان

٩. اواخر

١٠. اعلام

١١. اوراق

١٢. اغنية

نشاط ٢١ تدريب على قراءة الضمة	Activity 21 Practice reading *Damma* and
والكسرة على الهمزة والألف	*kasra* on *alif-hamza*

Practice reading these words aloud. Some words do not contain أُ or إِ to help you review other letters and sounds you have learned.

أُثْبِت   إناث   أُمَم   إن

يُحِب   إتْمام   وَزن   أُكْرِم

وَهبة   إجادة   إدارة

نشاط ٢٢ تدريب على الإملاء: الهمزة في	Activity 22 Dictation practice: *hamza* at
أول الكلمة	the beginning of words

Listen to the dictation words and write them down as precisely as you can in Arabic letters. Be sure to write the short vowels.

_____ .1

_____ .2

_____ .3

_____ .4

_____ .5

_____ .6

_____ .7

_____ .8

_____ .9

_____ .10

Like the short vowels and *sukuun*, this shape is one of the non-letter symbols that forms part of the Arabic writing system.

Name: شَدّة (*shadda*)

Sound: The word "*shadda*" means "strengthening" or "emphasis," and any consonant that has *shadda* written above it is pronounced for twice as long as normal. Another way to think about *shadda* is as something that "doubles" the letter it is above, as if there were actually two of the same letter in that spot. Listen to *shadda* in the following words and repeat them aloud.

عِلْمِيّ   حُرِّيّات   أَتَسَوَّق   أَيّام

Meaning: Does *shadda* have a particular meaning? Later, when you study Arabic roots and patterns, you will learn that *shadda* is extremely important for understanding the root of each word and for using an Arabic dictionary. For now, you just need to practice pronouncing *shadda* correctly. In many cases, however, *shadda* does affect the meaning of words. Look at these pairs of words whose meaning changes when you change the short vowels and add *shadda*:

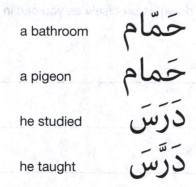

a bathroom	حَمّام
a pigeon	حَمام
he studied	دَرَسَ
he taught	دَرَّسَ

In other cases, words that have *shadda* have no meaning at all without *shadda*.

Shape: *shadda* is written directly above a consonant and is shaped like a small, slanted *w*, or a cartoon bird flapping its wings.

We recommend that you write شَدّة properly at all times and memorize it as part of the spelling when you learn a new word. In the long run, this will be extremely helpful for your pronunciation.

Some Arabic speakers do not use شَدّة when they write; for a native speaker, it is easy to know the pronunciation and meaning of a word even without seeing all the non-letter symbols written down. It is important to remember that شَدّة is always part of the words it belongs to, whether it is written or not, and must always be pronounced correctly—just like the short vowels.

When a short vowel comes after a letter that is emphasized by *shadda*, both symbols are written above the letter. This chart shows you how to combine *shadda* and the short vowels.

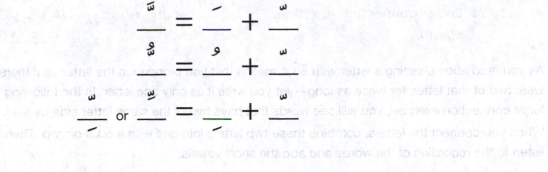

نشاط ٢٣ تدريب على كتابة الشدة

Practice writing *shadda* as many times as you can across one line.

ــّ

Now, write the following short words that contain *shadda* across each line, pronouncing it as you write.

جَدَّد

حَسَّ

العِزُّ

What does the shape of *shadda* remind you of? How will you help yourself remember its sound? Draw a picture or write some notes here:

Activity 24 Letter connection practice:
shadda

نشاط ٢٤   تدريب على ربط الحروف:
الشدة

As you read above, seeing a letter with شدّة means that you pronounce the letter as if there were *two* of that letter, for twice as long—yet you write it as only *one* letter. In the following letter connection exercise, you will see words that have two of the same letter side by side. When you connect the letters, combine these two letters into one with a شدّة on top. Then, listen to the recording of the words and add the short vowels.

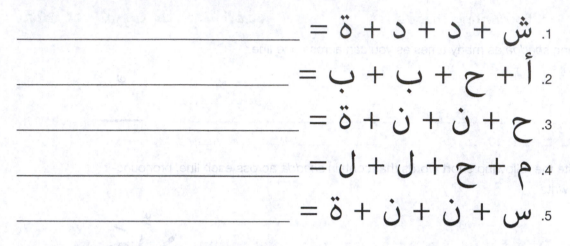

1. ش + د + د + ة = _____

2. أ + ح + ب + ب = _____

3. ح + ن + ن + ة = _____

4. م + ح + ل + ل = _____

5. س + ن + ن + ة = _____

Note: It is possible for some Arabic words to have the same consonant side by side, as long as they have a short vowel in between them.

نشاط ٢٥   تدريب على الاستماع: هل
هناك شدة؟

Activity 25 Listening practice: Is there
shadda?

Is there a شدّة on that word? Listen to the following list of words and mark whether you
think each one has شدّة on it or not.

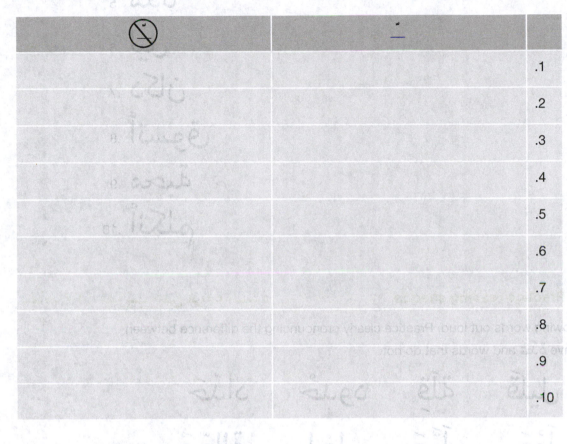

⌀ (shadda with slash)	ّ	
		.1
		.2
		.3
		.4
		.5
		.6
		.7
		.8
		.9
		.10

نشاط ٢٦   تدريب على الاستماع: أين
الشدة؟

Activity 26 Listening practice: Where is
shadda?

Now that you have practiced identifying whether or not there is a شدّة on different words,
practice listening for where شدّة occurs in different words. Read over the list of words to
familiarize yourself with them. You'll notice that none of them have short vowels or شدّة.
You will hear the words pronounced; fill in the short vowels and شدّة where you hear them.
Listen carefully: not all words have a شدّة on them! For example, if you were presented with
the word متوسط, you would add the vowels and شدّة to make it مُتَوَسِّط after hearing the
word.

١. مدرس

٢. تشرب

3. تشرفنا

4. أيام

5. مدة

6. ليل

7. دكان

8. أتسوق

9. محبة

10. أتكلم

Activity 27 Practice reading *shadda*

نشاط ٢٧   تدريب على قراءة الشدة

Read the following words out loud. Practice clearly pronouncing the difference between words that have شدّة and words that do not.

قَليل   قِلّة   حُدود   حَدّاد

حَوْلَ   حَوَّلَ   راحِل   رَحّالة

تَمييز   مُمَيِّز

REVIEW

المراجعة

Activity 28 Letter connection practice

نشاط ٢٨   تدريب على ربط الحروف

Connect the letters as appropriate to form words. Then listen to the recording of the words and add the short vowels that you hear.

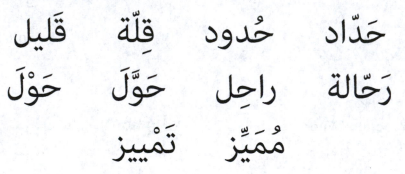

1. إ + ذ + ن = _____

2. ر + س + م + ي = _____

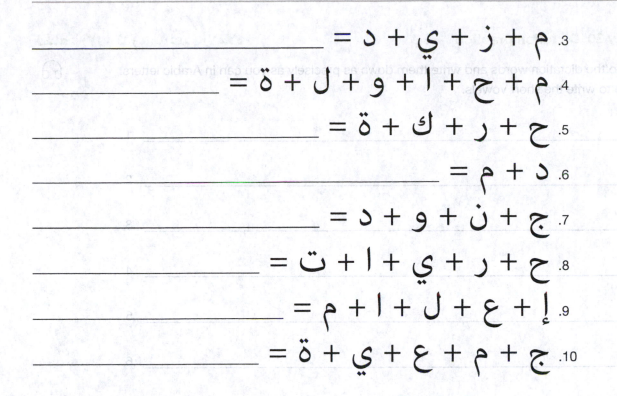

3. م + ز + ي + د = _____

4. م + ح + ا + و + ل + ة = _____

5. ح + ر + ك + ة = _____

6. د + م = _____

7. ج + ن + و + د = _____

8. ح + ر + ي + ا + ت = _____

9. إ + ع + ل + ا + م = _____

10. ج + م + ع + ي + ة = _____

Activity 29 Practice reading handwriting   نشاط ٢٩   تدريب على قراءة خط اليد

Practice reading these handwritten words out loud:

إذن   مَذهَب   ذاكِرة   عَشَرة   ثَلاثة

أُدرُس   أَتَكَلَّم   أُحِبّ   شِدَّة   أُمِّم

Activity 30 Dictation practice   نشاط ٣٠ تدريب على الإملاء

Listen to the dictation words and write them down as precisely as you can in Arabic letters.
Be sure to write the short vowels.

_____ ١.

_____ ٢.

_____ ٣.

_____ ٤.

_____ ٥.

_____ ٦.

_____ ٧.

_____ ٨.

_____ ٩.

Activity 31 Reading practice: World Cup 2014   نشاط ٣١ تدريب على القراءة: كأس العالم ٢٠١٤

Soccer is the most popular sport in the world, as well as the most popular sport in the
Middle East. But where do the best soccer teams come from? On the next page are the
eight starting groups for the FIFA 2014 World Cup. What countries can you recognize?
Keep a tally of how many countries come from each continent.

المجموعة الرابعة	المجموعة الثالثة	المجموعة الثانية	المجموعة الأولى
الأوروغواي	كولومبيا	إسبانيا	البرازيل
كوستاريكا	اليونان	هولندا	كرواتيا
إنجلترا	ساحل العاج	تشيلي	المكسيك
إيطاليا	اليابان	أستراليا	الكاميرون

المجموعة الثامنة	المجموعة السابعة	المجموعة السادسة	المجموعة الخامسة
بلجيكا	ألمانيا	الأرجنتين	سويسرا
الجزائر	البرتغال	البوسنة	فرنسا
روسيا	غانا	إيران	الإكوادور
كوريا الجنوبية	الولايات المتحدة	نيجيريا	هندوراس

قرعة نهائيات كأس العالم 2014

How many teams played in the World Cup from each continent? Keep a tally. (Try to read the continent names on your own, but you may need your teacher's help to understand the last two.)

أمريكا الشمالية	أمريكا الجنوبية	آسيا	أفريقيا	أوروبا	أستراليا

What would you guess the following words mean, from context?

1. مجموعة: _____

2. الولايات in الولايات المتّحدة (hint: look at the flag): _____

3. كوريا الجنوبية in الجنوبية: _____

Reflection: You may notice that although soccer is extremely popular in the Middle East, not many Middle Eastern teams played in the World Cup in 2014. What factors might affect a country's ability to put together a World Cup-level soccer team?

Activity 32 Reading practice: "The Voice"   نشاط ٣٢   تدريب على القراءة: "ذا فويس"

Practice reading *taa' marbuuTa* by examining this excerpt from the Wikipedia page about a reality TV show called "The Voice—أحلى صوت" that aired in 2012. For this exercise, do not expect to understand all or even most of it. Instead, follow the instructions to focus on what you *can* learn from the text. (In this case, you are focusing on *taa' marbuuTa*.) This exercise helps build the skills of guessing and inference that you will use throughout your Arabic learning career. Even though you do not know all of the letters yet, you can still get information from a real Arabic text!

1. Look at the text overall, focusing on the **formatting** and **images** to understand what you are seeing. Do not be distracted by trying to read letters yet. What can help you find the column that lists where each contestant is from?

2. Look at the column that lists where each contestant is from. The word next to each flag gives the contestant's nationality. Identify whether each contestant is male or female by looking for ة in that word. On a separate sheet of paper, make a tally of male and female contestants.

3. Which country has the most contestants in this round of the competition? Which country has the fewest? (If you are not sure about country names and flags, look up Arab country names and flags online or ask your teacher.)

4. Challenge question! What else can you identify in the article or the chart? While you do not know all of the letters yet, use guessing skills when you can to find familiar elements.

Hint 1: Look at the column titled الأغنية for English song titles written in Arabic letters. (Start with row numbers 5 and 9, and then see how many others you can find.)

Hint 2: Look next to the English song titles for singers whose names you know.

ذا فويس: أحلى صوت (الموسم الأول)
الحلقة الحادية عشر

النتيجة	الأغنية	الأصل	الاسم	المدرب	التسلسل
اختيار المدرب	"يا ضلي يا روحي، وائل كفوري"	مغربي	محمد عدلي		1
اختيار المدرب	"ما تجبش سيرتي، أنغام"	مصرية	إنجي أمين	شيرين عبد الوهاب	2
خرج من السباق	"يا بلادي، عزيز الشافعي ورامي جمال"	مصري	عبد العظيم الذهبي		3
اختيار الجمهور	"آي سيوتي بيغو، ميشيل تيلو"	مغربي	فريد غنام		4

النتيجة	الأغنية	الأصل	الاسم	المدرب	التسلسل
اختيار المدرب	"هيرو، إنريكيه إغليسياس"	لبناني	موري حاتم		5
اختيار المدرب	"وحشتني، سعاد محمد"	تونسي	حسان عمارة	عاصي الحلاني	6
خرج من السباق	"لبنان يا قطعة سما، وديع الصافي"	لبناني	إيلي أسمر		7
اختيار الجمهور	"علي جرى، عليا التونسية"	مغربي	مراد بوريقي		8
اختيار المدرب	"تايم تو سي غودباي، أندريا بوتشيلي"	سورية	نور عرقسوسي		9
خرجت من السباق	"فيرست بي أي ووومان، غلوريا غاينور"	لبنانية	ربى الخوري		10
اختيار المدرب	"أمباير ستيت أوف مايند، أليشيا كيز"	لبنانية	كريس جر	كاظم الساهر	11
اختيار الجمهور	"وين آي نيد يو، ليو سيير"	تونسية	يسرا محنوش		12

النتيجة	الأغنية	الأصل	الاسم	المدرب	التسلسل
اختيار المدرب	"بحلم بلقاك، ذكرى"	مغربية	لمياء الزايدي		13
اختيار المدرب	"غريبة الناس، وائل جسار"	مصري	سامر أبو طالب	صابر الرباعي	14
خرجت من السباق	"مين ده اللي نسيك، نانسي عجرم"	تونسية	لمياء جمال		15
اختيار الجمهور	"اللي نساك إنساه، عبد الله الرويشد"	عراقي	قصي حاتم		16

Adapted from "(الموسم 1) ذا فويس: أحلى صوت," Wikipedia, last modified May 6, 2020,

http://ar.wikipedia.org/wiki/(الموسم_الأول)_ذا_فويس:_أحلى_صوت

PART SIX

PART SIX GOALS

By the end of this section, you should be able to do the following:

- Read, write, pronounce, and connect the letters: ص ض ط ظ
- Recognize the difference between letters of the Arabic alphabet that often sound similar to English speakers
- Read, write, and pronounce *tanwiin al-fatH* at the end of common words: ‫أً‬

الجزء السادس

أهداف الجزء السادس

Letter name: صاد (*Saad*)

Sound: The sound of ص is similar to that of the letter س, but it is pronounced with your
tongue lower in your mouth, not touching the roof. For learners of Arabic, this sound
often takes practice to hear and pronounce appropriately. In this book, we represent
Saad in English letters with a capital "S."

Like the letter *raa'*, *Saad* is a letter that changes the quality of the vowels that are
near it. The easiest way to learn to hear ص is to listen for the deeper quality that ألف
and فتحة have when they fall near ص in a word. Listen to *Saad* in the following words
and repeat them aloud:

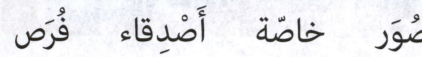

فُرَص   أَصْدِقاء   خاصّة   صُوَر

Social/antisocial: This letter is social.

Shapes: Look at the four forms of ص. Notice the small "tooth" above the line after the
large rounded shape.

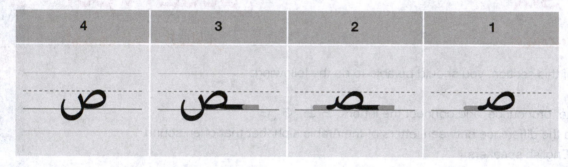

4	3	2	1
ص	ص	ـصـ	ص

Activity 1   Practice writing *Saad*   نشاط ١   تدريب على كتابة الصاد

Practice writing each form of ص as many times as you can across one line. Make sure to
write the small "tooth" to the left of the main loop. Say the sound aloud as you write it.

ص

What does this letter's appearance remind you of? How will you help yourself remember its sound? Draw a picture or write some notes here:

| Activity 2 | Letter connection practice: | نشاط ٢ | تدريب على ربط الحروف: |
| | *Saad* | | الصاد |

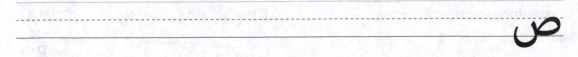

Connect the letters as appropriate to form words. Then listen to the recording of the words and add the short vowels that you hear.

١. ص + ص + ق = _____

٢. ب + ص + م + ة = _____

٣. ص + ف + ح + ة = _____

٤. ت + ص + ر + ي + ح = _____

٥. ن + ص + و + ص = _____

| Activity 3 | Listening practice: *Saad* vs. *siin* | نشاط ٣   تدريب على الاستماع: الصاد مقابل السين |

Practice hearing and recognizing the difference between the letters س and ص. You will hear a list of words. For each one, make a check mark in the column that represents the sound you heard in that word. For example, if you hear the word بسيط and you recognize the sound as a س, put a check in the س column.

س	ص	
		1.
		2.
		3.
		4.
		5.
		6.
		7.
		8.
		9.
		10.

| Activity 4   Practice reading *Saad* | نشاط ٤   تدريب على قراءة الصاد |

Practice reading these words containing ص and س out loud. Focus on pronouncing your new letters correctly.

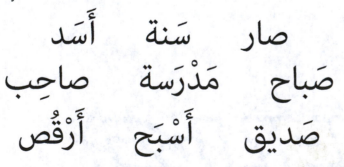

أَسَد   سَنة   صار

صَباح   مَدْرَسة   صاحِب

صَديق   أَسْبَح   أَرْقُص

Activity 5   Dictation practice: *Saad*   نشاط ٥   تدريب على الإملاء: الصاد

Listen to the dictation words and write them down as precisely as you can in Arabic letters.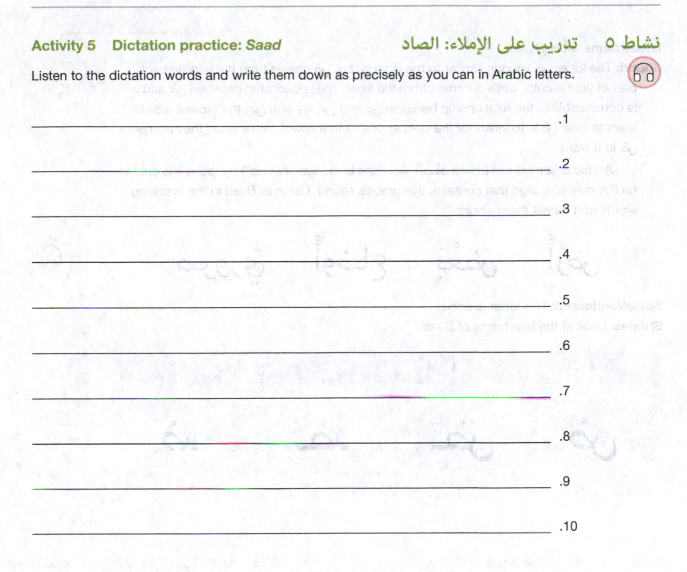

_____ .1

_____ .2

_____ .3

_____ .4

_____ .5

_____ .6

_____ .7

_____ .8

_____ .9

_____ .10

Activity 6   Practice reading *Saad* **and** *siin*   نشاط ٦   تدريب على قراءة الصاد
in context   والسين في جملة

This tongue twister will give you a lot of practice pronouncing the letters س and ص. Try to
read it as fast as you can—without letting your pronunciation get sloppy.

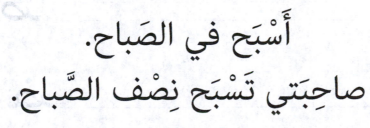

أَسْبَح في الصَّباح.
صاحِبَتي تَسْبَح نِصْف الصَّباح.

Can you figure out what this tongue twister means?

Letter name: ضاد (*Daad*)

Sound: The letter ض sounds similar to the letter د, but ض comes from the middle-back part of your mouth, while د comes from the front. The relationship between ض and د is comparable to the relationship between ص and س. As with ص, the easiest way to learn to hear ض is to listen for the deeper quality that vowels have when they fall near ض in a word.

Arabic is sometimes called لُغة الضّاد ("the language of *Daad*") because it is said to be the only language that contains this precise sound. Listen to *Daad* in the following words and repeat them aloud:

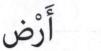 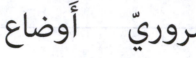

أَرْض   بَعْض   أوضاع   ضَروريّ

Social/antisocial: This letter is social.

Shapes: Look at the four forms of *Daad*:

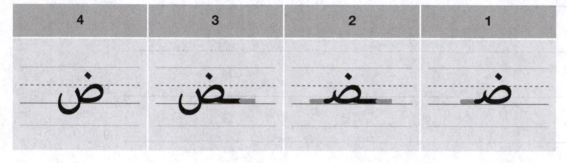

4	3	2	1
ض	ـض	ـضـ	ضـ

Activity 7   Practice writing *Daad*   تدريب على كتابة الضاد   ٧ نشاط

Now practice writing all four forms of ض. As with ص, make sure to write the small "tooth" on the left because this is what will make clear that you are writing ض and not another letter. Say the sound aloud as you write it.

ضـ

ـضـ

ـض

ض

What does this letter's appearance remind you of? How will you help yourself remember its sound? Draw a picture or write some notes here:

نشاط ٨	تدريب على القراءة: أين الحروف؟ (الضاد والصاد)	**Activity 8**	**Reading practice: Where are the letters? (*Daad* and *Saad*)**

Scan these lines from the poem "Al-Mutanabbi to Sayf al-Dawla" by the classical Arab poet al-Mutanabbi, and circle each instance you see of ض and ص. These lines are all from the same poem, but they do not necessarily come consecutively in the original.

وتصغر في عين العظيم العظائم   تعظُمُ في عين الصغير صغارها

وقد عجزت عنه الجيوش الخضارم   يكلّف سيف الدولة الجيش مَمَّه

وذلك ما لا تدّعين الضراغم   ويطلب عند الناس ما عند نفسه

How many do you see of each? ض: _____ ص: _____

نشاط ٩	تدريب على ربط الحروف: الضاد	**Activity 9**	**Letter connection practice: *Daad***

Connect the letters as appropriate to form words. Then listen to the recording of the words and add the short vowels that you hear.

١. م + ع + ر + ض = _____

٢. ي + خ + و + ض = _____

٣. ض + م + ة = _____

4. أ + ف + ض + ل = ــــــــــــــــــــــــــــــــــــ

5. و + ا + ض + ح = ــــــــــــــــــــــــــــــــــــ

Activity 10 Listening practice: *Daad* vs. *daal*   نشاط ١٠   تدريب على الاستماع: الضاد مقابل الدال

Practice hearing and recognizing the difference between the letters ض and د. You will hear a list of words. For each one, make a check mark in the column that represents the sound you heard in that word. For example, if you hear the word عضو and you recognize the sound as a ض, put a check in the ض column.

د	ض	
		.1
		.2
		.3
		.4
		.5
		.6
		.7
		.8
		.9
		.10

Activity 11 Practice reading *Daad*

نشاط ١١   تدريب على قراءة الضاد

Practice reading these words containing ض and د out loud. Focus on pronouncing your new letters correctly.

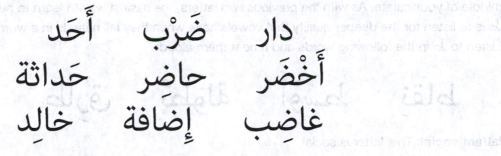

أَحَد   ضَرْب   دار

حَداثة   حاضِر   أخْضَر

خالِد   إضافة   غاضِب

Activity 12 Dictation practice: *Daad*

نشاط ١٢   تدريب على الإملاء: الضاد

Listen to the dictation words and write them down as precisely as you can in Arabic letters.

_____ 1.

_____ 2.

_____ 3.

_____ 4.

_____ 5.

_____ 6.

_____ 7.

_____ 8.

_____ 9.

_____ 10.

Letter name: طاء (*Taa'*)

Sound: The letter ط sounds similar to the letter ت, but ت is articulated with the tip of the tongue at the front of your palate, while ط falls on the middle of the tongue and the middle of your palate. As with the previous two letters, the easiest way to learn to hear ط is to listen for the deeper quality that vowels have when they fall near ط in a word. Listen to ط in the following words and repeat them aloud:

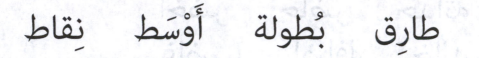

نِقاط   أَوْسَط   بُطولة   طارِق

Social/antisocial: This letter is social.

Shape: The letter ط is a social letter than can take the following four shapes. What similarities and differences do you notice between the shapes of this letter and those of ص?

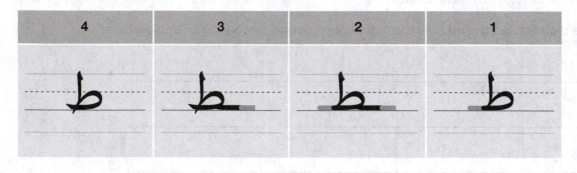

4	3	2	1
ط	ط	ط	ط

Activity 13 Practice writing *Taa'*   نشاط ١٣   تدريب على كتابة الطاء

Now practice writing all four forms of ط. Make sure to write the tall vertical piece of the ط after the rest of the word you are writing, the way you dot the letter *i* or cross the letter *t* when writing in cursive. Say the sound aloud as you write it.

What does this letter's appearance remind you of? How will you help yourself remember its sound? Draw a picture or write some notes here:

Activity 14 Letter connection practice: *Taa'*

نشاط ١٤   تدريب على ربط الحروف: الطاء

Connect the letters as appropriate to form words. Then listen to the recording of the words and add the short vowels that you hear.

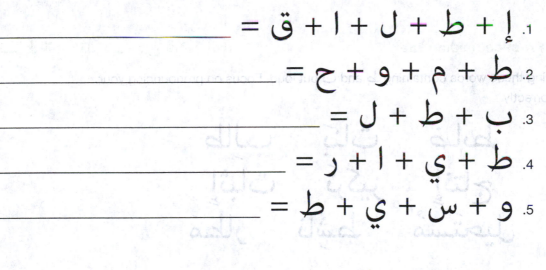

$$\text{.1} \quad = \text{ق} + \text{ا} + \text{ل} + \text{ط} + \text{إ} \quad \rule{3cm}{0.4pt}$$

$$\text{.2} \quad = \text{ح} + \text{و} + \text{م} + \text{ط} \quad \rule{3cm}{0.4pt}$$

$$\text{.3} \quad = \text{ل} + \text{ط} + \text{ب} \quad \rule{3cm}{0.4pt}$$

$$\text{.4} \quad = \text{ر} + \text{ا} + \text{ي} + \text{ط} \quad \rule{3cm}{0.4pt}$$

$$\text{.5} \quad = \text{ط} + \text{ي} + \text{س} + \text{و} \quad \rule{3cm}{0.4pt}$$

Activity 15 Listening practice: *Taa'* vs. *taa'*

نشاط ١٥   تدريب على الاستماع: الطاء مقابل التاء

Practice hearing and recognizing the difference between the letters ط and ت. You will hear a list of words. For each one, make a check mark in the column that represents the sound you heard in that word. For example, if you hear the word عطر and you recognize the sound as a ط, put a check in the ط column.

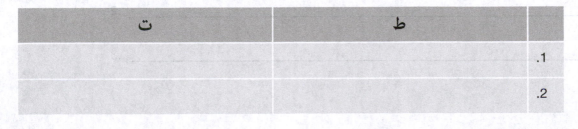

ت	ط	
		.1
		.2

ت	ط	
		.3
		.4
		.5
		.6
		.7
		.8
		.9
		.10

Activity 16 Practice reading *Taa'*

تدريب على قراءة الطاء   نشاط ١٦

Practice reading these words containing ط and ت out loud. Focus on pronouncing your new letters correctly.

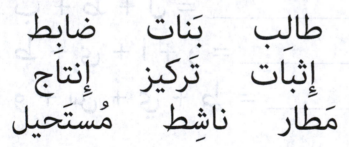

طالب   بَنات   ضابِط
إثبَات   تَركيز   إنتاج
مَطار   ناشِط   مُستَحيل

Activity 17 Dictation practice: *Taa'*

تدريب على الإملاء: الطاء   نشاط ١٧

Listen to the dictation words and write them down as precisely as you can in Arabic letters.

_____ .1

_____ .2

_____ .3

_____ .4

_____ .5

_____ .6

_____ .7

_____ .8

_____ .9

_____ .10

Activity 18 Practice reading *Taa'* in context

نشاط ١٨   تدريب على قراءة الطاء في جملة

This tongue twister will help you practice pronouncing the new letter ط while reviewing the sounds of ح and خ. Try to read it as fast as you can without letting your pronunciation get sloppy.

خَيط حَرير عَلى حَيط خَليل

It means, "a silk string on Khalil's wall."

Letter name: ظاء (*DHaa'*)

Sound: The letter ظ sounds similar to the letter ذ, but ذ comes from the tip of your tongue and the front of your palate, while ظ comes from the middle of your tongue and the middle of your palate. As with previous letters, the easiest way to learn to hear ظ is to listen for the deeper quality that vowels have when they fall near ظ in a word. Listen to *DHaa'* in the following words and repeat them aloud:

ظاهِر   نِظام   يَظَلّ   مُحافِظ

Social/antisocial: This letter is social.

Shapes: Review the four forms of ظ:

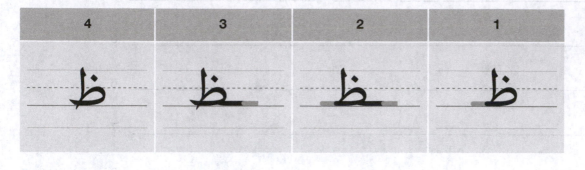

4	3	2	1
ظ	ظ	ظ	ظ

Activity 19 Practice writing DHaa'   نشاط ١٩   تدريب على كتابة الظاء

Now practice writing all four forms of ظ. Say the sound aloud as you write it.

What does this letter's appearance remind you of? How will you help yourself remember its sound? Draw a picture or write some notes here:

Activity 20 **Letter connection practice:** *DHaa'*	نشاط ٢٠ تدريب على ربط الحروف: الظاء

Connect the letters as appropriate to form words. Then listen to the recording of the words and add the short vowels that you hear.

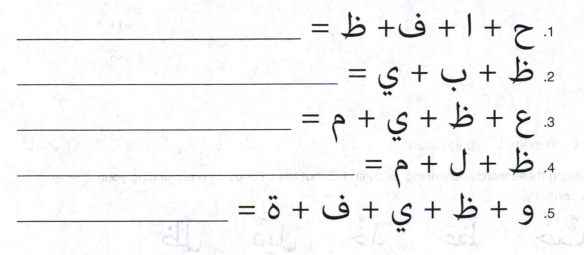

$$\text{ح} + \text{ا} + \text{ف} + \text{ظ} = \underline{\hspace{4cm}} \quad .1$$

$$\text{ظ} + \text{ب} + \text{ي} = \underline{\hspace{4cm}} \quad .2$$

$$\text{م} + \text{ظ} + \text{ي} + \text{ع} = \underline{\hspace{4cm}} \quad .3$$

$$\text{م} + \text{ظ} + \text{ل} + \text{م} = \underline{\hspace{4cm}} \quad .4$$

$$\text{و} + \text{ظ} + \text{ي} + \text{ف} + \text{ة} = \underline{\hspace{4cm}} \quad .5$$

Activity 21 **Listening practice:** *DHaa'* vs. *dhaal* and *thaa'*	نشاط ٢١ تدريب على الاستماع: الظاء مقابل الذال والثاء

Practice hearing and recognizing the difference between the letters ظ, ذ, and ث. You will hear a list of words. For each one, make a check mark in the column that represents the sound you heard in that word. For example, if you hear the word عذّر and you recognize the sound as a ذ, put a check in the ذ column.

ث	ذ	ظ	
			.1
			.2
			.3
			.4
			.5
			.6
			.7
			.8

ث	ذ	ظ	
			9.
			10.
			11.
			12.

Activity 22 Practice reading *DHaa'*

نشاط ٢٢   تدريب على قراءة الظاء

Practice reading these words containing ظ, ذ, and ث out loud. Focus on pronouncing your new letters correctly.

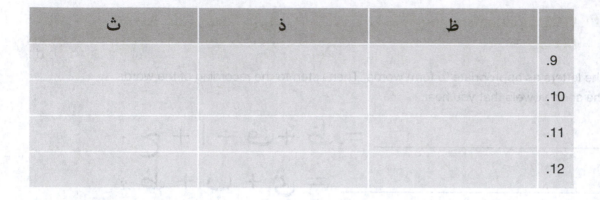

ظِلّ   ذَيل   خُذ   حَظّ   حَثّ

اِنتِظار   مَظهَر   مَذهَب   مُحافِظة

Activity 23 Dictation practice: *DHaa'*

نشاط ٢٣   تدريب على الإملاء: الظاء

Listen to the dictation words and write them down as precisely as you can in Arabic letters.

_____ 1.

_____ 2.

_____ 3.

_____ 4.

_____ 5.

_____ 6.

_____ 7.

_____ .8

_____ .9

_____ .10

CONGRATULATIONS!

مَبروك!

You have reached the last letter of the Arabic alphabet, with just a few more non-letter symbols to learn!

أَ

In this section you will learn about another non-letter symbol: *tanwiin al-fatH*. This is not part of the alphabet, yet it has a distinctive sound and grammatical meaning. It is another component of Arabic writing, along with the short vowels (ـَ ـُ ـِ). We are introducing *tanwiin al-fatH* now because it appears commonly in spoken Arabic and everyday texts.

Symbol name: تَنْوين الفَتْح (tanwiin al-fatH)

Sound: *tanwiin al-fatH* makes the sound of a short *fatHa* vowel followed by the letter نون. It only appears at the end of words. When you hear this *an* sound at the end of a word, you are usually (but not always) hearing the *tanwiin al-fatH* sound, not the letter ن. ("tanwiin" literally means to make a *nuun*, and so "tanwiin al-fatH" means to add a *nuun* sound to a *fatHa*.) Listen to *tanwiin al-fatH* in the following words and repeat them aloud:

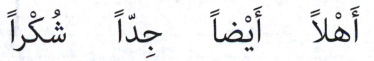

شُكْراً   جِدّاً   أَيْضاً   أَهْلاً

Shapes: the shape of *tanwiin al-fatH* is made up of two *fatHa* shapes written at the end of a word. On most words, you must add a letter ا at the end of the word for *tanwiin al-fatH* to "sit on." This letter ا here is just a platform for *tanwiin al-fatH* and it does **not have a sound of its own** when used like this.

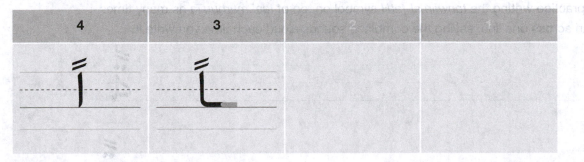

4	3	2	1
أً	أً		

Sometimes, people do not write or print the two *fatHa* shapes on words that have *tanwiin al-fatH*. However, the letter *alif* that is a platform for *tanwiin al-fatH* is **always** written. For example, each pair of words below is pronounced exactly the same, even though the vowels and *tanwiin* are not written on the second word.

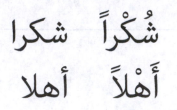

There are some cases where you do not need to add ‍ﺍ as a platform for *tanwiin al-fatH*. For example, if a word ends in ة, there is no need to add the letter ‍ﺍ as a platform. Write the *tanwiin al-fatH* symbol directly above the ة and pronounce the combined sound: *atan*, with two short *fatHa* vowel sounds. Practice reading these words aloud:

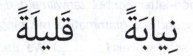

Activity 24   Practice writing *tanwiin al-fatH*   نشاط ٢٤   تدريب على كتابة تنوين الفتح

Practice writing the *tanwiin al-fatH* symbol over each form of the ‍ﺍ platform as many times as you can across one line, saying the sound aloud each time you write it.

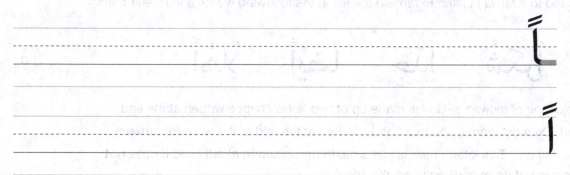

Now practice writing the *tanwiin al-fatH* symbol on top of *taa' marbuuTa* as many times as you can across one line, saying the combined sounds aloud each time you write it.

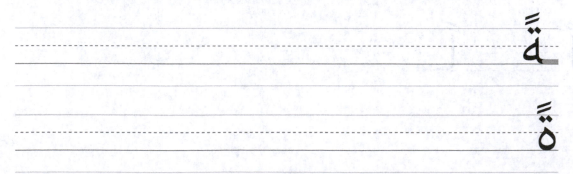

What does the appearance of *tanwiin al-fatH* remind you of? How will you help yourself remember its sound? Draw a picture or write some notes here:

Activity 25 Writing and reading practice:
** *tanwiin al-fatH***

نشاط ٢٥   تدريب على الكتابة والقراءة:
تنوين الفتح

First, read the words in the right column aloud. Then, to the left of the word, rewrite the word and add *tanwiin al-fatH* to the end of it, making the appropriate additions or changes as necessary. Finally, read the words you have written aloud.

1. سابِق
_____

2. نَوْع
_____

3. مَثَل
_____

4. كَثيرة
_____

5. عِلْم
_____

6. قَليل
_____

7. مُمْكِنة
_____

8. تَمام
_____

Activity 26 Dictation practice:
   tanwiin al-fatH

نشاط ٢٦ تدريب على الإملاء:
تنوين الفتح

Listen to the dictation words and write them down as precisely as you can in Arabic letters. Remember, if you hear what sounds like a letter نون after the vowel *fatHa* at the end of the word, you can assume that is *tanwiin al-fatH*.

_____ .1

_____ .2

_____ .3

_____ .4

_____ .5

_____ .6

_____ .7

_____ .8

_____ .9

_____ .10

    To learn more about some common uses of *tanwiin al-fatH*, complete Activity 32 in the review and expansion activities that follow.

REVIEW AND EXPANSION   المراجعة والتوسيع

Activity 27 Reading and listening practice: نشاط ٢٧ تدريب على القراءة والاستماع:
   Similar words   كلمات متشابهة

In this exercise, you will read a number of similar words in the same line. Your teacher will read one of those words aloud; circle the one that you hear them read.

    The goal of this exercise is to help you review the fine distinctions between Arabic letter sounds, check your own reading abilities, and help you identify letters whose sound you may need to review.

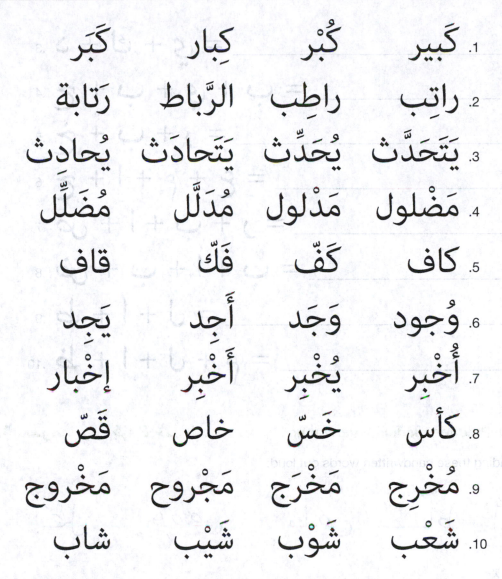

1. كَبير   كُبْر   كِبار   كَبَر

2. راتِب   راطِب   الرِّباط   رَتابة

3. يَتَحَدَّث   يُحَدِّث   يَتَحادَث   يُحادِث

4. مَضْلول   مَدْلول   مُدَلَّل   مُضَلَّل

5. كاف   كَفّ   فَكّ   قاف

6. وُجود   وَجَد   أَجِد   يَجِد

7. أُخْبِر   يُخْبِر   أَخْبِر   إخْبار

8. كَأس   خَسّ   خاص   قَصّ

9. مُخْرِج   مَخْرَج   مَجْروح   مَخْروج

10. شَعْب   شَوْب   شَيْب   شاب

Reflection: Look over the exercise above. What letters or letter combinations did you struggle with the most? Make a note of them to yourself here:

_____

Activity 28 Letter connection practice   نشاط ٢٨   تدريب على ربط الحروف

Connect the letters as appropriate to form words. Then listen to the recording of the words and add the short vowels that you hear.

1. ذ + ل = _____

2. أ + ز + ر + ا + ر = _____

3. ذ + ي + ك + ذ = _____

4. ح + ب + ي + ب = _____

5. خ + ب + ر = _____

6. ج + ا + م + ع = _____

7. ص + ا + ب + ر = _____

8. ض + ا + ب + ب = _____

9. ط + ا + ل = _____

10. ظ + ا + ل + م = _____

Activity 29 Practice reading handwriting   نشاط ٢٩   تدريب على قراءة خط اليد

Practice reading these handwritten words out loud:

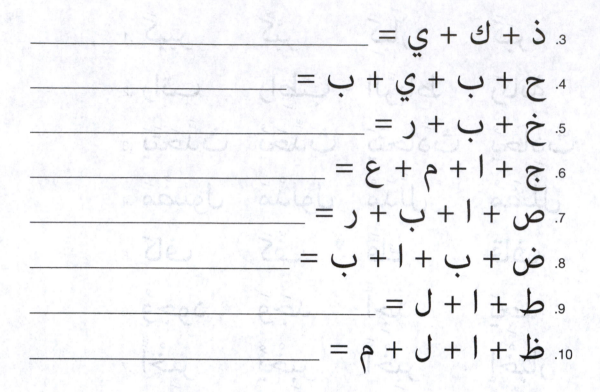

Activity 30 Reading and listening practice: نشاط ٣٠   تدريب على القراءة والاستماع:
Similar words   الكلمات المتشابهة

In this exercise, you will read a number of similar words across each row (similar to Activity 27). Then your teacher will read one of those words aloud. Choose the word that you hear from a line of words with similar sounds. Use this as a chance to check your progress on the letters that you identified in Activity 27 as difficult for you.

1. زَمَن سَمَن زَمان رُمّان

2. سَعْد صاد صاعِد سَعيد

3. تَغْليل تَخْليل تَعْليل تَخْليل

4. ثَبات ثابِت ثُبوت ثَبَت

5. شُكوك شَكّاك شِقاق شَقيق

6. خُذ حَظّ خَطّ حَثّ

7. بَيض باض بَعْد بَعْض

8. يُرسِل يُراسِل يَتَرَسَّل يَتَراسِل

9. غَريب راغِب خَرْب خَراب

10. وِسادة أُسْرة يُسْرة عُسْرة

Activity 31 Dictation practice نشاط ٣١ تدريب على الإملاء 🎧

Listen to the dictation words and write them down as precisely as you can in Arabic letters.

_____ 1.

_____ 2.

_____ 3.

_____ 4.

_____ 5.

_____ .6

_____ .7

_____ .8

_____ .9

_____ .10

Activity 32 Writing practice: _tanwiin al-fatH_ in context   نشاط ٣٢ تدريب على الكتابة: تنوين الفتح في الكلمات

Look at the beginning of these common words containing _tanwiin al-fatH_ that you may have already heard in conversation. Say the words aloud, and then complete the spelling of each word using اً at the end. If you aren't sure what the words should sound like, ask your teacher for help.

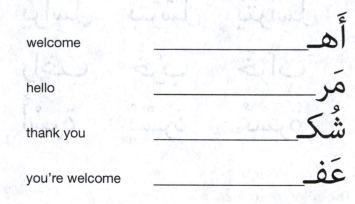

welcome _____ أَهـ

hello _____ مَر

thank you _____ شُكـ

you're welcome _____ عَفـ

LETTER SOUNDS IN ARABIC DIALECTS   أصوات الحروف في اللهجات العربية

Have you ever learned a form of English in school that is different from the way you speak? For example, many schools teach that contractions like "can't" and "don't" are appropriate for talking and informal writing, while "cannot" and "do not" are more appropriate for formal written situations. This is an example of different varieties of English being used in different situations. Similarly, Arabic has both a formal variety (called _al-fuSHaa_, or Modern Standard Arabic) and many informal varieties.

If you were listening to the news or reading a book in an Arabic-speaking country, you would typically encounter _al-fuSHaa_. (Be careful: in this transliterated spelling of الفُصحى the _S_ and _H_ are two different letters and sounds, not an _sh_ sound—so make sure to pronounce it *al-fuS-Haa*.) On the other hand, if you were chatting with Arabic-speaking friends, buying groceries in a market, or bargaining for a souvenir, it would be typical for you to speak an informal variety, or "dialect." While similar to concepts like "accent" or "slang" in English, the term "dialect" is used to describe an informal variety of Arabic that is used in a particular country or region. The Arabic term for an informal variety is "*al-ᶜaammiyya*," and this variety is like the everyday English you use all the time without even thinking about it.

Have you ever had trouble understanding native English speakers of English who grew up in another country, or another region of your country? Chances are that this difficulty was caused by differences in regional dialect. These can include differences in accents, vocabulary, and grammar. For instance, an English speaker from North America may have trouble understanding an English speaker from Australia if she uses slang that is common in Australia but not in North America or just pronounces familiar words in an unfamiliar way. The different dialects of Arabic *ᶜaammiyya*, spoken by majorities in more than twenty countries, are also regional and differ in terms of vocabulary, pronunciation, and grammar.

Standard Arabic, or *al-fuSHaa*, is the variety used in more formal situations and across all of the Arabic-speaking world in essentially the same way, from Morocco to Iraq. On the other hand, the varieties of Arabic *ᶜaammiyya* are used in everyday situations and are different from country to country. So why doesn't everyone just communicate in *al-fuSHaa* all the time? Well, no one speaks *al-fuSHaa* as a native language, meaning that many people cannot speak this variety spontaneously, though they can often understand it well. What's more, the fact that this shared variety is associated with written and formal situations means that for many people, *al-fuSHaa* seems stodgy: imagine if instead of saying, "Mom, I'm gonna go to the mall," you were to say, "Mother, I shall go to the shopping center." At the same time, many Arabic speakers place great importance on learning and using *al-fuSHaa*, as it is the language of Arabic literature and a shared cultural heritage that goes back many centuries.

In different spoken Arabic varieties, some letters are pronounced differently from their *fuSHaa* pronunciation. The *Jusuur* textbook exposes you to some of these differences with a focus on Levantine spoken varieties. Levantine Arabic is spoken in the Levant, a region

that includes Jordan, Palestine, Israel, Syria, and Lebanon. When you encounter Levantine Arabic in *Jusuur*, you will hear letters pronounced differently from their pronunciation in *al-fuSHaa*.

Where a dialect originates and where speakers of that dialect reside do not always align. Accordingly, in the discussion of "urban" and "rural" varieties that follows, it is important to keep in mind that these labels refer only to the varieties' places of origin—not necessarily those of speakers. Indeed, in capital cities such as Amman, Jordan, it is common to hear multiple varieties, since communities of speakers have moved to the city from a variety of areas inside and outside of Jordan.

The letter *qaaf* in Arabic dialects 　　　　　حرف القاف في اللهجات العربية

The letter ق varies a lot between different varieties. In fact, speakers of many of the major Arabic dialect families pronounce the letter ق completely differently from its formal Arabic pronunciation.

- Many urban varieties in the eastern Arab world (in the cities of Jerusalem, Damascus, and Beirut, for example) pronounce ق as a glottal stop, which is the sound of *hamza* (ء). You have learned about ء at the beginning of a word (أ) in Part One. At the middle or end of a word it represents a total stop of all sounds, like that in the middle of *uh-oh* or *batboy*. To make this sound, just close all the muscles of your throat for an instant. For example, in these dialects the word قَليل is pronounced *'aliil* and the word يَقوم is pronounced *ya'uum*.
- Some rural (sometimes called Bedouin) varieties in the eastern Arab world (from the villages and countryside in Jordan, for example) pronounce ق as a hard *g* sound, like in *bug*. For example, in these varieties the word قَليل is pronounced *galiil* and the word يَقوم is pronounced *yaguum*.

When working on alphabet drills in this book, you are expected to use the *fuSHaa* pronunciation of ق. In Part Seven you will, however, see some words or phrases in purple, indicating that the corresponding audio recording uses the Levantine variety for pronunciation. It is important to train your ear to recognize the different pronunciations of this letter. Being able to hear the differences will help you recognize familiar words spoken by speakers of different varieties.

Activity 33 Listening practice: The letter *qaaf* in Arabic dialects

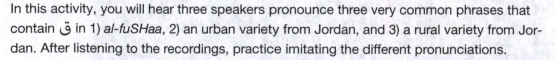

نشاط ٣٣ تدريب على الاستماع: حرف القاف في اللهجات العربية

In this activity, you will hear three speakers pronounce three very common phrases that contain ق in 1) *al-fuSHaa*, 2) an urban variety from Jordan, and 3) a rural variety from Jordan. After listening to the recordings, practice imitating the different pronunciations.

"O my heart, ..." ("Sweetheart, ...")	"At the same time ..."	"She said to me ..."	
يا قلبي	في نفس الوقت	قالَت لي	A person speaking al-fuSHaa
يا قلبي	بِنفس الوقت	قالَت لي	A person who grew up in Amman, Jordan, whose parents are originally from Jerusalem (a major urban center)
يا قلبي	بِنفس الوقت	قالَت لي	A person from Mafraq, Jordan (a rural Jordanian town)

The letters *thaa'*, *dhaal*, and *DHaa'* in Arabic dialects

حروف الظاء والذال والثاء في اللهجات العربية

These three letters differ in pronunciation from *al-fuSHaa* in some, but not all, of the Levantine varieties.

- In many rural or Bedouin varieties, these letters are pronounced exactly like the *fuSHaa* pronunciation.
- In many varieties, the sounds of these letters change, sometimes into one sound and sometimes into another.

   In this book and in the *Jusuur* textbook, we always write informal variety words in their *fuSHaa* spelling, even when they include letters whose pronunciation is different in the informal variety. We do this to emphasize the commonality between *al-fuSHaa* and the informal varieties.

Urban Levantine Pronunciation	*fuSHaa* Letter and Pronunciation
ت	ث
س	
د	ذ
ز	
ز	ظ

Activity 34 Listening practice: The letters *DHaa'*, *dhal*, and *thaa'* in informal Arabic varieties

نشاط ٣٤   تدريب على الاستماع: حروف الظاء والذال والثاء في اللهجات العربية

In this drill, you will hear three speakers pronounce five common words that contain ث, ذ, and ظ in 1) *al-fuSHaa*, 2) an urban variety from Jordan, and 3) a rural variety from Jordan. After listening to the recordings, practice imitating the different pronunciations.

"conditions"	"clever"	"melts"	"seconds"	"much"	
ظُروف	ذكي	يَذوب	ثَواني	كَثير	A person speaking *al-fuSHaa*
ظُروف (ز)	ذكي (ز)	يَذوب (د)	ثَواني (س)	كثير (ت)	A person who grew up in Amman, Jordan, whose parents are originally from Jerusalem (a major urban center)
ظُروف	ذكي	يَذوب	ثَواني	كثير	A person from Mafraq, Jordan (a rural Jordanian town)

Ask your teacher what other varieties they are familiar with and how letter sounds change in those varieties. Then practice saying some words you know in those varieties.

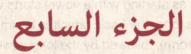

PART SEVEN
الجزء السابع

Across the previous sections, you learned all of the letters and sounds of the Arabic alphabet, as well as several symbols. In this section, you will learn how to write, recognize, and pronounce a number of additional symbols and special letters that play an important role in Arabic script but do not involve any new sounds.

PART SEVEN GOALS
أهداف الجزء السابع

By the end of this section, you should be able to do the following:

- Recognize, write, and pronounce the variants of *hamza* occurring at the beginning of a word: أ أُ إ آ أُو إِبـ أ
- Recognize, write, and pronounce الـ correctly
- Recognize, write, and pronounce the variants of *hamza* occurring in the middle or at the end of a word: ؤ ئ أ ء
- Recognize, write, and pronounce the other varieties of *alif*: ـَىٰ
- Recognize, write, and pronounce all kinds of *tanwiin*: أ ةٌ ـٌ ـٍ

You have already learned how to write *hamza* when combined with a **short vowel** at the beginning of a word: it is always written on an *alif* "seat." Reminder: *alif* here is **not a long vowel**; rather, it is a "platform" for the *hamza*. Practice the pronunciation of initial *hamza* in the following words:

أُسْطورة   إِخْوة   أَطْفال

أَفْضَل   أُصول   إِبْراز

Check your pronunciation with your classmates and your teacher.

Now, you will expand your knowledge to understand how *hamza* combines with **long vowels** at the beginning of words. Remember that any word that English speakers would think of as starting with a vowel starts with a form of *hamza* in the Arabic script. When that vowel is long, the basic principle is simple: write the *hamza* as you normally would (on an *alif* platform), followed by the long vowel. (Within Arabic script, *hamza* is considered to be a unique sound that can be followed by any vowel, just like any other consonant.) Writing this *hamza* + long vowel combination is straightforward when it comes to representing the long vowel sounds *uu* and *ii* at the beginning of words:

When *hamza* is followed by a long *aa* sound, a new rule comes into play: writing two *alifs* next to each other is **not** allowed in the Arabic script. Therefore, we write the combination of a *hamza* and a long *aa* vowel as a single *alif* shape with a special symbol above it:

$$آ = ١ + أ$$

The wavy line symbol is called مَدَّة (meaning "extension") and only appears above ١.
Whenever you see it, you know there will be a long *alif* sound, not the short vowel indicated
when ء is written above ١. This combination of *alif* symbols into *alif madda* also occurs
when two *hamzas* appear next to each other at the beginning of a word:

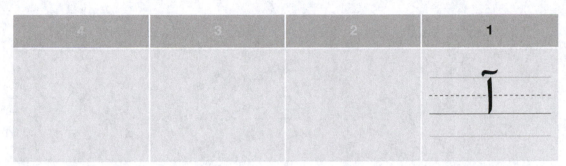

4	3	2	1
			آ

Listen to the initial *hamza* with long vowels in the following words and repeat them
aloud:

إِيمان   أُوروبا   آنَ   إِيقاف

| نشاط ١ | تدريب على كتابة الهمزة وحروف المد في أول الكلمة | **Activity 1** | **Practice writing *hamza* and the long vowels at the beginning of words** |

Practice writing *alif madda* and each other combination of *hamza* + long vowel as many
times as you can across one line, saying the sound aloud each time you write. Remember
that long vowels in Arabic take up at least twice as much time as short vowels.

أُو

إِيـ

آ

The only new symbol you have learned here is *alif madda*. What does this combination's appearance remind you of? How will you help yourself remember its sound? Draw a picture and write some notes here:

Activity 2	Reading and listening practice: *hamza* at the beginning of words	نشاط ٢ تدريب على القراءة والاستماع: الهمزة في أول الكلمة

In this drill you will practice distinguishing between different types of *hamza* at the beginning of words.

Before listening   قبل الاستماع

Read aloud the words in the list below. Pay attention to whether the *hamza* at the beginning of each word is followed by a short vowel or a long vowel, and whether it is part of a diphthong sound such as *aw* or *ay*. Check your pronunciations with your classmates and teacher.

١. آنَ   أَنا

٢. أَميل   إيـمَيل

٣. أُولاها   أُلّاهي

٤. إيـمان   أَيْـمَن

٥. أُرْبة   أُوروبا

٦. آمين   أَمين

٧. أَوْضاع   أُوضة

Listening

الاستماع

Now, listen to the recording of the seven words and circle the word you hear from each pair.

After listening

بعد الاستماع

After reviewing the correct answers, work with a classmate and challenge your reading and listening skills. Let one partner choose a word at random and read it aloud; then let the other partner point to the word they heard on their own page. Check whether you got it right, then switch roles and repeat.

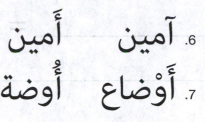

Activity 3 Letter connection practice: *hamza* **and** *madda*	<div dir="rtl">نشاط ٣ تدريب على ربط الحروف: الهمزة والمدة</div>

Connect the letters as appropriate to form words, leaving the first ا in each word unadorned. Then listen to the recording, write the correct symbol (*hamza* or *madda*) in the correct position, and add the short vowels that you hear.

١. ا + و + ك + ي = ــــــــــــــــــــــ

٢. ا + ي + ص + ا + ل = ــــــــــــــــــــــ

٣. ا + ي + د + ي = ــــــــــــــــــــــ

٤. ا + ض + ا + ف = ــــــــــــــــــــــ

٥. ا + ل + ا + م = ــــــــــــــــــــــ

٦. ا + ر + د + ن + ي = ــــــــــــــــــــــ

٧. ا + ف + ر + ي + ق + ي = ــــــــــــــــــــــ

٨. ا + ي + ر + ا + ن = ــــــــــــــــــــــ

9. ‫ا + و + ج + ا + ع‬ = _____

10. ‫ا + د + ب‬ = _____

Activity 4   Dictation practice: *hamza* **and**   نشاط ٤   تدريب على الإملاء: الهمزة
              madda   والمدة

Listen to the dictation words and write them down as precisely as you can in Arabic letters:

_____ 1.

_____ 2.

_____ 3.

_____ 4.

_____ 5.

_____ 6.

_____ 7.

_____ 8.

_____ 9.

a	10	موكـــا
a ICE	10	موكــا آيس
hocolate	10	هوت شوكـلـت
ccino	10	كابتشيــنــو
ccino ICE	10	كابتشيــنــو آيس

Name: همزة الوصل (hamzat al-waSl)

Sound: There is another kind of *hamza* that appears at the beginning of words called همزة الوصل, or "connecting *hamza*." In brief, this is a *hamza* that is pronounced at the beginning of sentences or phrases, but not in the middle of them. Rather, in the middle of sentences, همزة الوصل seamlessly "connects" the sounds of the letters it occurs between, without the usual "stop" sound of the *hamza*.

Listen to همزة الوصل as it occurs when written as ا in الـ in the expressions below (notice that there is no *hamza* shape written). Practice speaking each expression aloud.

البَيْت　　　في البَيْت

الأُسْتاذ　　مَعَ الأُسْتاذ

Notice the difference in the pronunciation of the همزة الوصل in الـ when it occurs at the start of an expression versus when it occurs in the middle of an expression: When البَيْت is pronounced by itself, the همزة الوصل in الـ occurs at the start of an expression. Accordingly, it is pronounced like a normal *hamza*. By contrast, when البَيْت is pronounced as part of the expression في البَيْت, the همزة الوصل in الـ occurs in the middle of an utterance, after a word. In this case, همزة الوصل makes no sound itself but rather connects the sound that precedes it to the sound that follows it; the two words في البَيْت are elided together, without any pause or "stop" sound between them. Making sure that there are no such pauses between words in Arabic (unless there is a regular *hamza* written as ء) is important for making your speech sound smooth and correct.

Shape: The connecting *hamza* is always written as an *alif*, and the ء shape is never written with it. By far the most common appearance of the connecting *hamza* in Arabic is the ا of الـ, the definite article. The ا shape for the connecting *hamza* is always written, even when it has no sound.

To learn more about other uses of همزة الوصل and the special shape that is sometimes written with it, please turn to the end of Part Seven.

Activity 5　Listening practice: Connecting *hamza*　　نشاط ٥　تدريب على الاستماع: همزة الوصل

In this activity, you will practice writing and reading aloud phrases and sentences that include الـ in the middle. Listen to the examples on the next page.

Note: Example phrases are given in both العامية and الفصحى. Though some of the short vowels are different between these two registers, both varieties require that words be connected smoothly without pausing. As in the *Jusuur* textbook, the purple text represents العامية الشامية, while the blue text represents الفصحى.

English	العامية الشامية	الفصحى
The big house is in the city	البَيت الْكَبِير في المَدينة	البَيْتُ الْكَبِيرُ في الْمَدينة
The father works in the restaurant and the office	الأَب بيشْتَغِل في المَطْعَم والمَكْتَبة	الأَبُ يَعْمَلُ في الْمَطْعَمِ وَالْمَكْتَبة
The busy mother likes coffee with milk	الإمّ الْمَشْغولة بِتْحِبّ الْقَهْوة بِالْحَليب	الأُمُّ الْمَشْغولَةُ تُحِبُّ الْقَهْوَةَ بِالْحَليب

Notice that the reader does not pause between words, and that the ا in الـ does not make a *hamza* (glottal stop) sound, except at the very beginning of each sentence. Practice reading the sentences above yourself *without stopping* between words. Reading and speaking this way is an important part of fluency in all varieties of Arabic.

Activity 6   **Writing and reading practice:**   نشاط ٦   تدريب على الكتابة والقراءة:
             Connecting *hamza*   همزة الوصل

Using the words below, create your own simple phrases or sentences to practice. Use linking words such as و and في and بـ to connect words. After you have written your phrases, practice reading them aloud and share them with your classmates or teacher.

Adjectives	People	Locations	Things	Linking Words
المشغول	الأم	المول	القهوة	وَ
الجميل	الأب	المكتبة	الحليب	في
الحلو	الأخ	العمل	الماء \ المي	بـ
القصير	الأخت	المدينة	الكتاب	
الكبير		البيت		
		المطعم		
		المدرسة		

_____ .1

_____ .2

_____ .3

4.

_____

5.

_____

نشاط ٧   تدريب على الإملاء: همزة الوصل   **Activity 7   Dictation practice: Connecting hamza**

When you write sentences that you hear, you will have to get used to "hearing" the الـ of words even when the ا sound is not audible. In Activity 6 we saw the phrase في المدينة. You will hear this as *fil-madiina*, but you must write it as two separate words. In this dictation activity, there are some phrases that start with بـ, وَ, or في. Be careful, not all of the words in this activity start with الـ! (Note that there is no space between وَ or بـ and the words that come after them because they are one-letter words.)

_____ 1.

_____ 2.

_____ 3.

_____ 4.

_____ 5.

_____ 6.

_____ 7.

_____ 8.

ALIF-LAAM AND THE SUN AND MOON LETTERS

أَلِف-لام والحروف الشمسية والقمرية

Activity 8   Reading practice: Words with alif-laam

نشاط ٨   تدريب على القراءة: كلمات فيها ألف-لام

You have already been exposed to الـ (the definite article in Arabic) in a number of words and phrases. Some of those words and phrases are in the word cloud below.

Can you find phrases from the following categories? Write as many as you see.

Phrases used in greetings: _____

Days of the week: _____

Times of day: _____

Phrases used with verbs: _____

Sports: _____

Beverages: _____

كرة القدم

يوم الثلاثاء

القهوة

الحمد لله

كرة السلة

السلام عليكم

الشاي

من الممكن

المساء

الصباح

من اللازم

يوم الأحد

Activity 9 Listening practice: *alif-laam* in words	نشاط ٩ تدريب على الاستماع: ألف-لام
	في الكلمات
Listening	الاستماع

Listen and read along to these words from the word cloud, with and without الـ:

Word with الـ	Word without الـ
الحَمْد	حَمْد .1
الأَحَد	أَحَد .2
المَساء	مَساء .3
المُمْكِن	مُمْكِن .4
القَدَم	قَدَم .5
القَهْوة	قَهْوة .6
السَلام	سَلام .7
الثُلاثاء	ثُلاثاء .8
الصَباح	صَباح .9
اللازِم	لازِم .10
السَلّة	سَلّة .11
الشاي	شاي .12

After Listening بعد الاستماع

What do you notice about the way that الـ is pronounced in words 7–12? In these words, the لـ sound disappears and the first letter of the word, written after لـ, is now twice as long, as if it had a *shadda* on it. Even though there is no longer a لـ sound, the لـ in الـ is still written. This pronunciation change happens with half of the Arabic consonants, while the other half of the consonants make no change to the pronunciation of الـ.

Activity 10 Reading practice: *alif-laam* in Latin letters

نشاط ١٠ تدريب على القراءة: ألف-لام في الحروف اللاتينية

Look through the following authentic examples of people writing Arabic on social media using Latin letters rather than Arabic letters. Find words you already know that have الـ and the sound change in them. (Hint: look for doubled letters in words that start with an *a*.) Work with a classmate and follow these steps:

1. Circle the words that you find.
2. Copy the word in Roman script.
3. Guess how to write the word in Arabic script, using الـ.

Word in Arabic Script (use الـ)	Word in Roman Script		
		Fayrouz Sho7ror Assabaa7... beautiful voice, will never die!!	.1
		"Everything happens because a reason .. Don't blame others for that kind of reason .." #Assalamualaikum #MorningWednesday	.2
		wallah ila twahhachnaha bazzaf..allah yaatik assahha aala had ssouwar	.3

Activity 11 Listening practice: Sun and moon letters

نشاط ١١ تدريب على الاستماع: الحروف الشمسية والقمرية

One way to identify the letters that change the pronunciation of الـ is to pay attention to where the sounds of these letters are produced in your mouth. In general, most letters pronounced by touching your tongue to your teeth or near the front of the roof of your mouth are letters that change the pronunciation of الـ. As a class, say the Arabic consonants aloud and sort them into their appropriate category (one letter per box) with the help of your teacher.

				أ
خ	ح	ج	ث ت ب	د
ص ش س ز ر ذ				
ق ف غ ظ ط				
ي و هـ ن م ل ك ض				

الحُروف القَمَرِيّة Letters that do not change the pronunciation of الـ	الحُروف الشَّمْسِيّة Letters that change the pronunciation of الـ

Check your work with your teacher before proceeding!

Sun and moon letters

الحروف الشمسية والقمرية

The traditional names for these groups of letters are the "sun letters" (الحروف الشمسية) and the "moon letters" (الحروف القمرية) because the Arabic words for "sun" and "moon" each start with a letter of the two different types. For each letter, you will have to memorize whether it is a sun letter or a moon letter.

When the first letter of a word is a sun letter, we write a *shadda* on top of that first letter. This *shadda* is not normally written, but we write it while learning a word to remind ourselves of the different pronunciation.

السَّلام　　　الـ + سَلام

When the first letter of a word is a moon letter, we write a *sukuun* on top of the ل of the الـ. This *sukuun* is a reminder of the pronunciation.

الْمَدينة　　الـ + مَدينة

Activity 12　Writing and reading practice: Adding *alif-laam* to words

نشاط ١٢　تدريب على الكتابة والقراءة: إضافة الألف-لام إلى الكلمات

1. Identify the first letter of each word below as a "sun" or "moon" letter and draw a corresponding sun or moon symbol next to it.
2. Rewrite the word with الـ added to the beginning. Include all of the short vowels. Make sure to write *shadda* or *sukuun* according to the first letter.
3. Practice reading the new words aloud. Record yourself reading the first 10 of the words aloud and send the recording to your teacher.

١. وِلاية

_____

٢. صَباح

_____

٣. شَهْر

_____

٤. جَيِّد

_____

٥. زَوْجة

_____

٦. ظُهْر

_____

٧. كَثير

_____

٨. طَويل

_____

٩. رَقْم

_____

10. ساعة _____

11. مَساء _____

12. يَوْم _____

13. بَيْت _____

14. نَهار _____

15. هِواية _____

16. صاحِب _____

17. حَبيبة _____

18. مُمتاز _____

19. ذكيّ _____

20. تَلَفِزْيون _____

نشاط ١٣ تدريب على القراءة والاستماع:	**Activity 13 Reading and listening practice:**
كلمات متشابهة	**Similar words**

It is very important to be able to hear whether a word has ال at the beginning or not. The presence or absence of ال usually changes the meaning of the sentence completely.

1. For each row, read each of the words aloud and notice the differences between each one.
2. Listen to the recording of each word and circle the word in the row that you hear.

1. السَّلَم   أَسْلَم   السَّلام

2. الذَّكي   أَذْكِياء   أَذْكى

3. الشَّرْق   أَشْرَقَ   شَرْق

4. أَفْلام   الفيلْم   الفُلان

5. السَّماء   أَسْماء   أَسْمى

6. أَصْحاب   أَسْحَب   السَّحاب

7. أَنْعَم   النَّعمة   نَعَم

Activity 14 Dictation practice: Sun and moon letters	نشاط ١٤ تدريب على الإملاء: الحروف الشمسية والقمرية 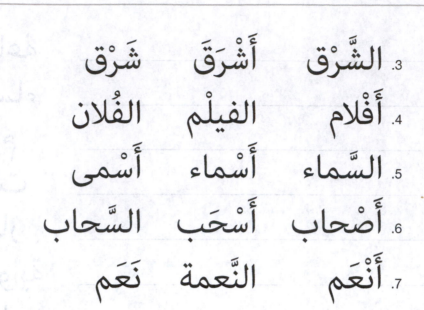

In this exercise, write the words that you hear. Some of them have الـ and some do not; some of them begin with sun letters and some begin with moon letters. Listen carefully!

_____ 1.

_____ 2.

_____ 3.

_____ 4.

_____ 5.

_____ 6.

القطرانة

الكرك

مؤتة

المزار الجنوبي

You have already learned about the sound of همزة (ء). You learned that it always appears on an *alif* at the beginning of a word and that it sounds differently depending on the vowels that go with it. Now, you will learn to write and recognize *hamza* when it appears in the middle and at the end of words.

Sound: The sound of a همزة in the middle of a word represents a stopping of the flow of air before and after a vowel. In English, this is like the stop of air that happens when we say, *uh-oh*. Sometimes, when speaking English, we make the همزة sound instead of the letter *t*, as in *Batman* or *rotten*. Practice saying these words and the همزة sound aloud.

Shapes: In the middle and at the end of a word, همزة appears in a number of different forms. Which form it appears in and which letter it sits on depends on a series of rules that you do not need to know at this stage; for now, focus on recognizing and pronouncing همزة in its different positions. When you learn a word that has همزة in it, you must memorize the spelling for that particular word. Unlike writing short vowels, writing همزة is not optional!

The symbol *hamza* can appear on the different shapes of the letters ي, و, and ا; it can also appear by itself sitting on the line:

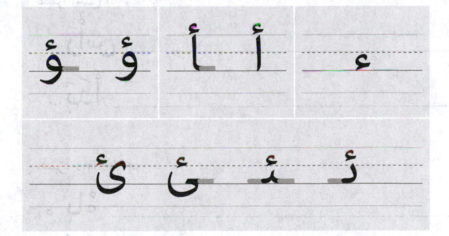

Notice that when *hamza* sits on the shape of ى, there are no dots written. Remember that these symbols are not vowels but rather just "platforms" to hold the همزة. Just like a consonant, these ways of writing همزة can be followed by any of the long or short vowels.

Activity 15 Writing practice: *hamza* at the middle and end of words

نشاط ١٥   تدريب على الكتابة: الهمزة في وسط الكلمة وآخرها

First listen to the recording of the following words and repeat them aloud after the recording. Then practice writing همزة in various forms by copying each of these words as many times as you can along each line, reading the word as you write.

همزة على ى

1. رَئيس _____

2. مِئات _____

3. شاطِئ _____

همزة على و

4. رُؤوس _____

5. مُؤْتَمَر _____

همزة على ا

6. رَأْس _____

7. بَدَأً _____

on the line همزة

8. باءْ _____

9. أَسْماء _____

10. لِقاءات _____

Activity 16 Reading and listening practice:
         Similar words with *hamza*

نشاط ١٦   تدريب القراءة والاستماع:
كلمات متشابهة ذات همزة

In this activity, you will practice distinguishing words that include همزة and other sounds.

Before listening

Read aloud each word in the chart below, making sure to notice the differences in spelling and pronunciation between the words in each row. Check your pronunciation with your teacher.

شَريعة	شِراء	١. شارِع
سائِل	سُعال	٢. سُؤال
بَرّ	بَعْر	٣. بِئر
عَسّاف	عَسَف	٤. أَسَف
عَقيد	عَقِد	٥. أَكيد
مَأمون	مَعْمول	٦. مَأمول

Listening

You will hear one word from each of the rows in part أ. Circle the word that you hear and review your choice with your teacher.

After listening

After reviewing the correct responses, work with a classmate and challenge each other's reading and listening skills. Let one partner choose a word at random and read it aloud; then let the other partner point to the word they heard in their own copy of the book. Check whether they got it right, then switch roles!

Activity 17 Letter connection practice: نشاط ١٧   تدريب على ربط الحروف:
hamza   الهمزة

First, connect the letters to form complete words. Then, listen to the recording and write in همزة where you hear it, at the beginning, middle, or end of a word. If you hear همزة at the end of a word, you will have to write it on the line. When you are done, listen again and write all of the short vowels and سكون on the words.

1. ل + و + و + س + م = _____

2. ت + ى + ش = _____

3. ١ + ر + ز + و = _____

4. ي + ١ + د + ي = _____

5. ق + ى + ١ + ق + ح = _____

6. ل + ١ + و + س = _____

7. ١ + ي + ز + ١ = _____

8. ي + ت + ١ + ي = _____

There are two more ways to write the long ا sound in Arabic that you will learn now. They are not part of the alphabet since they have the exact same pronunciation as the regular ا that you learned about in the first chapter. It is important that you know how to recognize and pronounce them.

Name: ألف مقصورة *(alif maqsuura)*

Sound: This letter makes the exact same sound as a long *alif* vowel. The name ألف مقصورة simply means "shortened alif." It appears only at the end of words. Listen to *alif maqsuura* in the following words and repeat them aloud:

قُرى   مَعْنى   أَدّى   تَمَنّى

Shape: This letter looks exactly like the letter ي but with two important differences: it has no dots and it only appears at the end of words. This means it only has two different shapes:

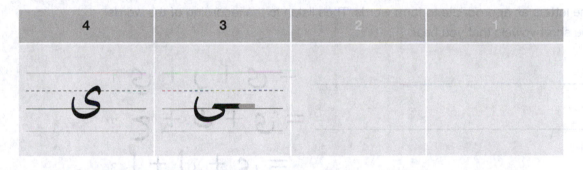

4	3	2	1
ى	ـى		

As you learn more words that end in the long ا sound, you will notice that some words are written with ا and some with ى. When you learn a new word, memorize which letter to use.

Activity 18 Practice writing *alif maqsuura*   نشاط ١٨   تدريب على كتابة الألف المقصورة

A. Listen to the recording of words ending in ألف مقصورة and say them each aloud a number of times as you follow along.

B. Write the short vowels and other "extra" symbols that you hear.

C. Practice writing *alif maqsuura* in various forms by copying each of these words three times.

١. على _____

٢. إحدى _____

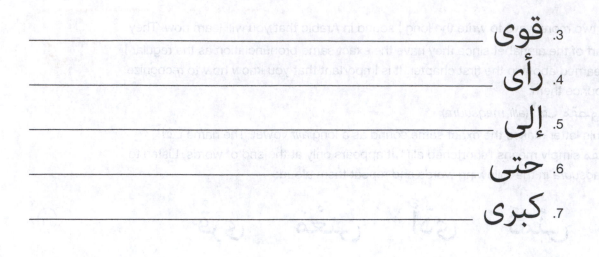

٣. قوى _____

٤. رأى _____

٥. إلى _____

٦. حتى _____

٧. كبرى _____

| Activity 19   Letter connection practice:
      alif maqsuura | نشاط ١٩   تدريب على ربط الحروف:
الألف المقصورة |

Connect the letters as appropriate to form words. Then listen to the recording of the words and add the short vowels that you hear.

١. ي + ر + ى = _____

٢. ح + ك + ى = _____

٣. إ + ل + ى = _____

٤. ي + ب + ق + ى = _____

٥. م + س + ت + و + ى = _____

٦. أ + ع + ل + ى = _____

| Activity 20   Writing and reading practice:
      alif maqsuura in "on" and "to" | نشاط ٢٠   تدريب على الكتابة والقراءة:
الألف المقصورة في "على" و
"إلى" |

Writing   الكتابة

The most common words that end in ألف مقصورة are the prepositions عَلى ("on") and إلى ("to"). Below, write four short sentences that include the phrases على الـ and إلى الـ and draw a small picture for each to show its meaning. Example: أذهب إلى البيت

١. _____

_____ 2.

_____ 3.

_____ 4.

Reading   القراءة

Practice reading your sentences aloud. Make sure to pay attention to the pronunciation of الـ. Review the sections about connecting *hamza* and sun and moon letters. If your teacher asks you to, record your sentences and submit them to your teacher for evaluation.

Name: ألف خنجرية (*alif khanjariyya*)

Sound: *alif khanjariyya*, or "dagger *alif*" in English, has the sound of a long-vowel *alif*. It appears in a small number of words. Listen to dagger *alif* in the following words and repeat them aloud.

هٰؤُلاء   اللّٰه   كَذٰلِكَ   الرَّحْمٰن

Shape: This symbol is not a letter that connects, but rather one of the extra shapes (along with the short vowels) that help in pronunciation and are often not written. It looks like a small independent *alif* floating above the letter whose sound it comes after. Now is a good time to learn and memorize the spelling and pronunciation of the common words that have a dagger *alif* in them—you already know several of them.

Activity 21   Listening practice: نشاط ٢١   تدريب على الاستماع:
       Dagger *alif*   الألف الخنجرية

Listen to the following words that have dagger *alif* in them. Now say them aloud as you follow along with the recording.

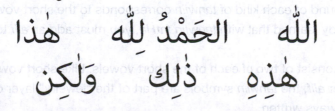

هٰذا   لِلّٰه   الحَمْدُ   اللّٰه

وَلٰكِن   ذٰلِك   هٰذِهِ

The other words that have dagger *alif* are rarer than these six words.

Activity 22 **Practice writing dagger *alif* in**   نشاط ٢٢ تدريب على كتابة الألف
              words   الخنجرية في كلمات

Next to their English translations in the diagram below, practice writing the common words
containing dagger *alif* both with and without the dagger *alif.* Remember that even if the
dagger *alif* is not written, it will still be pronounced as a long, extended *alif* sound.

		Written with dagger *alif*	Written without dagger *alif*
1.	this (*f.*)		
2.	but, however		
3.	God		
4.	this (*m.*)		
5.	Praise God		
6.	that (*m.*)		

You have already learned how to write and pronounce *tanwiin fatHa* (اً), which comes at the
end of many words. Now you will learn about the other kinds of *tanwiin* and how to write
and pronounce all of them.

Name: تَنوين (*tanwiin*)

Sound: There are three different kinds of *tanwiin*, one for each short vowel sound. *tanwiin*
only comes at the end of words, and it represents a short vowel (*a, u,* or *i*) followed by
the sound of ن. Listen to the three different kinds of *tanwiin* at the end of the word بيت
and repeat them aloud.

تنوين كسرة	تنوين ضمة	تنوين فتحة	
بَيْتٍ	بَيْتٌ	بَيْتاً	بَيْت

As you can hear, the sound of each kind of *tanwiin* corresponds to the short vowel
that it resembles. You already learned that with *tanwiin fatHa*, you must add an *alif* to
the end of the word.

Shape: The shapes of *tanwiin* consist of two of each of the short vowels. Like short vowels,
sukuun, shadda, and dagger *alif,* the *tanwiin* symbols are part of the "jewelry" layer of
Arabic script and are not always written.

Meaning: Adding *tanwiin* to a noun or adjective does not change the basic meaning of it. In the examples above, all three versions of the word بيت mean "a house" in English. The difference between them is grammatical: words take different *tanwiin* endings depending on the role, like subject or object, they play in a sentence. It may help to think of *tanwiin* as a kind of uniform that words wear to indicate what job they do in a sentence. For now, though, you only need to know how to recognize and pronounce *tanwiin* when you see it, not what the extra meaning of the symbol is.

Tanwiin and other short vowels appearing at the end of words are generally a feature of very formal Arabic prose, poetry, and speech. In most situations, even when speaking الفصحى formally, Arabic speakers do not pronounce these short vowel endings. However, they are still used to hearing them in formal religious language, political speeches, and recited poetry. These endings are also used in many children's books and cartoons on television.

Activity 23 Practice writing *tanwiin*   نشاط ٢٣   تدريب على كتابة التنوين

Practice writing and saying the three types of *tanwiin* on these words:

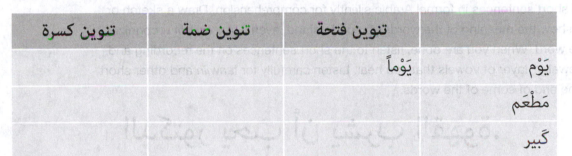

تنوين كسرة	تنوين ضمة	تنوين فتحة	
		يَوْماً	يَوْم
			مَطْعَم
			كَبير

When *tanwiin* is added to words that end in ة, the ة is pronounced as a ت. Note that you do not need to add *alif* when adding *tanwiin fatHa* to ة. Listen to the following example and then add *tanwiin* to these familiar words.

تنوين كسرة	تنوين ضمة	تنوين فتحة	
مَدينةٍ	مَدينةٌ	مَدينةً	مَدينة
			ساعة
			حَبيبة
			صَغيرة

Activity 24 Listening practice: *tanwiin* and final short vowels in sentences

نشاط ٢٤   تدريب على الاستماع: التنوين والحركات في جمل

Read these short sentences in formal Arabic silently for comprehension. Draw a sketch or diagram to show the meaning of the words you understand, even if you do not recognize every single word. When you are done, listen to the short sentences on the recording and write the "jewelry" layer of vowels that you hear. Listen carefully for *tanwiin* and other short vowels at the end of some of the words.

١. الدكتور يحب أن يشرب القهوة.

٢. هل تلعب كرة القدم كثيرا؟

٣. أريد صاحبا ممتازا.

4. هل تسكنين في ولاية كبيرة؟

5. بيتي صغير ولكنه جميل أيضا.

نشاط ٢٥   تدريب على قراءة التنوين في   Activity 25 Practice reading *tanwiin* in
جملة   context

Read the following tongue twister, taken from a poem by the famous poet Abu aT-Tayyib al-Mutanabbi (915–965 CE):

أَلَمٌّ أَلَمَّ أَلَمْ أُلِمَّ بِدَائِهِ   إِنْ آنَ آنٌ آنَ آنَ أُنُ أَوَانِهِ

Practice reading this line aloud as fast as you can, paying close attention to the vowels at the end of each word. It means: "I've got pain, but I don't know the disease; if it hurts me, it should be healed."

Activity 26 Practice reading handwriting

نشاط ٢٦   تدريب على قراءة خط اليد

Practice reading these handwritten words out loud:

Earlier in this chapter, you learned about how the همزة in الـ is not pronounced when in the middle of a sentence. Here, you will learn more about the different kinds of همزة that appear as the first letter in words.

أ

    Every word that begins with a همزة contains either همزة الوصل ("connecting *hamza*") or همزة القطع ("cutting *hamza*"). Most of what you have seen so far is همزة القطع—we call it this because the sound of the همزة literally cuts the stream of air in the middle of a phrase.

Activity 27 Listening drill: Different kinds of hamza

نشاط ٢٧   تدريب على الاستماع: همزة القطع وهمزة الوصل

Listen to these examples of phrases that contain a word beginning with همزة القطع:

١. فِي أُسْبوعٍ سَبْعَةُ أَيّام

٢. ثَلاثَة ثُمَّ أَرْبعة

    همزة الوصل on the other hand, **is often not pronounced at all**; it usually connects the vowel that comes before the همزة to the consonant that comes after it. Listen to these examples of phrases that contain a word that begins with همزة الوصل—you will hear that there is no break and the words flow together.

٣. فِي اسْـمي حَرْفُ الميم

٤. واحِد ثُمَّ اثْنَيْن

The reason this is called a همزة in the first place is that we do **sometimes** pronounce it as a همزة sound (glottal stop). This happens when همزة الوصل (which is always at the beginning of a word) comes at the beginning of a sentence:

5. اِسْمي طَويل

6. اِثْنَيْن وَعِشْرين

This همزة sound is also pronounced when these words come after الـ:

7. الاِسْم

8. الاِثْنَيْن

Listen to all of these examples again and speak each phrase aloud after you hear it.

Activity 28 Practice writing connecting
hamza

نشاط ٢٨   تدريب على كتابة همزة الوصل

In example phrases 3 and 4 of Activity 27, you may have noticed that even though no _hamza_ or long vowel sound is pronounced, an _alif_ is still written. This is true for all words containing همزة الوصل: the _alif_ shape is always written.

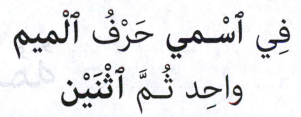

The symbol that we sometimes use to indicate همزة الوصل is a looping shape written above ا.

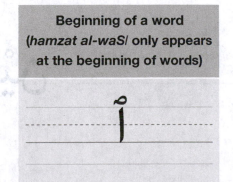

Beginning of a word
(_hamzat al-waSl_ only appears
at the beginning of words)

This symbol is usually only written in very formal texts. Practice writing the وصلة shape above an *alif*:

أ

In practice, همزة الوصل is usually written as an ‏ا‏ with no symbols on it at all. Practice writing these phrases containing common words that begin with همزة الوصل, and read them aloud as you write.

كَتَبَ اسْمَهُ

فِي الْبَيْت

دَرَسْتُ اثْنَيْن

When these words with همزة الوصل appear at the beginning of a sentence (or after الـ) and the همزة is pronounced, the appropriate short vowel is written with an ‏ا‏, but without a ء symbol.

اِسْمُهُ

اَلْبَيْت

الاِثْنَيْن

This is in contrast to words that begin with همزة القطع, which always has one of these symbols on it:

آ إ أ

Keeping track of the difference between these kinds of همزة is difficult even for native speakers of Arabic, so it is understandable if it takes you some time to learn this part of the Arabic alphabet. Here is an overview of the things to know about همزة at the beginning of a word:

1. Every word that starts with (what you hear as) a vowel sound actually starts with a همزة

2. همزة at the beginning of a word is **always** written using an ا (which is not a long vowel)

3. Every همزة starting a word is either همزة القطع (cutting) or همزة الوصل (connecting)

4. همزة القطع is always pronounced. It is always written with a ء shape above or below ا (or as the آ symbol)

5. همزة الوصل is pronounced at the beginning of sentences, but not in the middle of sentences

    a. When pronounced, the short vowel only is written above or below ا

    b. When not pronounced, only ا is written (or ٱ)

When you learn a new word that starts with ا, learn whether it starts with همزة القطع or همزة الوصل. Always write the correct همزة shape (أ إ آ) in words containing همزة القطع. This will help you to remember to pronounce it every time.

CONGRATULATIONS!

Give yourself a pat on the back—you have finished learning all the letters *and* symbols of the Arabic alphabet and script. It is an impressive feat and an important step toward becoming proficient in Arabic.

It is normal to continue to struggle with Arabic letter sounds and pronunciation. Most people who learn a language as adults will always have a foreign accent but still can improve their pronunciation to the point where native speakers can easily understand them. Listen to Arabic speakers' pronunciation and imitate it as closely as possible. When you receive a new vocabulary list, listen to the words and read them at the same time—this will help you continue to connect the letter sounds with the letters themselves. In time, your grasp of each letter and its sound will be good enough to pronounce new words correctly without hearing an Arabic speaker say them first.

It is also normal if Arabic script is still difficult for you. With practice, you will be able to read and write more quickly. The best way to become better at writing in Arabic is to use the script in your writing as much as possible. Practice the script in class and outside of class as well. Show your family and friends who do not study Arabic how to write their names in Arabic. Follow an Arabic account on social media and sound out the words even if you do not know what they mean. Partner with a friend in your Arabic class and text each other in Arabic.

By knowing the Arabic alphabet, you have opened the door to a language spoken by hundreds of millions of people worldwide and to a rich array of cultural traditions extending back centuries. Walk through the door and enjoy the rest of your journey!

Art credits

All images not attributed were taken by Sarah Standish, Richard Cozzens, or Rana Abdul-Aziz or are in the public domain.

All handwriting samples are by Lana Iskandarani, © 2022 Georgetown University Press.

PART ONE

Man writing Arabic calligraphy, p. 1: Flickr user Land Rover MENA. Creative Commons license: Attribution 2.0 Generic (CC BY 2.0).

Silhouettes holding hands, p. 3: Illustration by Christopher W. Totten, © 2022 Georgetown University Press.

Silhouettes holding hands with a break in the line: Illustration by Christopher W. Totten, © 2022 Georgetown University Press.

Arabic Ikea building, p. 15: Flickr user Paul Pehrson. Creative Commons Attribution license: 2.0 Generic (CC BY 2.0).

PART THREE

Writing on stone, p. 84: © 2022 Qatar Foundation International. Used with permission.

PART FOUR

Pizza, p. 115: Flickr user Katrin Gilger. Creative Commons license: Attribution-ShareAlike 2.0 Generic (CC BY-SA 2.0).

Pasta, p. 115: Flickr user Erik Stattin. Creative Commons license: Attribution- ShareAlike 2.0 Generic (CC BY-SA 2.0).

Salad, p. 115: Flickr user Junya Ogura. Creative Commons Attribution license: 2.0 Generic (CC BY 2.0).

Burger, p. 115: Flickr user Stu Spivack. Creative Commons license: Attribution- ShareAlike 2.0 Generic (CC BY-SA 2.0).

Two cans of Pepsi, p. 115: Flickr user medea_material. Creative Commons license: Attribution 2.0 Generic (CC BY 2.0).

PART SIX

Souq, p. 187: Adobe Stock user Mirek Hejnicki. Used with permission.

PART SEVEN

Moon, p. 203: Illustration by Christopher W. Totten, © 2022 Georgetown University Press.

Sun, p. 203: Illustration by Christopher W. Totten, © 2022 Georgetown University Press.

Yellow road sign in a desert, p. 215: Flickr user Mario Micklisch. Creative Commons license: Attribution 2.0 Generic (CC BY 2.0).

About the Authors

Sarah Standish was the founding teacher of the first high school Arabic program in the state of Oregon and also served as deputy director at OneWorld Now! in Seattle, Washington. She is the author of *Culture Smart! Syria*.

Richard Cozzens is a preceptor in Arabic at Harvard University and has served as the director of the STARTALK Arabic Summer Academy in Boston, Massachusetts. He has taught Arabic to high school and university students since 2008.

Rana Abdul-Aziz is a senior lecturer and the Arabic language coordinator at Tufts University. She has been teaching Arabic at various institutions and training new Arabic teachers for more than fifteen years.